MW00738107

Recipes
Tips
&
Tricks

Cooking For Two
in a
Confined Space

by Susan Maza

A product of Type 'N $ave™ software.

Copyright © 2002
Morris Press Cookbooks

Printed in the U.S.A. by

MORRIS PRESS
COOKBOOKS
P.O. Box 2110 • Kearney, NE 68848
800-445-6621 • www.morriscookbooks.com

Introduction

My home economics/consumer sciences background has naturally led me to the composition of this book. However, my years of RVing have added practical experience that my college schooling didn't provide. Each of these backgrounds has been added to my love of creative cooking. This cookbook is intended to be helpful to those who want to be more efficient with food and utensils used in the kitchen or galley. It is a guide for the Rver, boater and those living in "scaled-down residences" who would like to cook delicious, appealing meals for one or two people in a very limited space. Some of the recipes cannot be successfully reduced to produce an acceptable dish, thus you will see a larger quantity noted.

The recipes utilize basic food staples in a variety of ways to create simple, delicious meals from scratch. Very few convenience (proportioned or prepackaged) foods are used because they are generally more expensive and aren't as flavorful or healthy as freshly prepared foods. Basic food staples offer greater variety and more flexibility in diets.

Tips and recipe variations are sprinkled throughout the book to assist the cook in creating dishes that are interesting not only to eat but also to prepare.

The next few pages list basic utensils and how to best utilize them to economize space. Your list may be somewhat different based on your cooking needs. My rule of thumb is, "Never have anything that doesn't have at least two uses." You will also find a list of food staples you should always have on hand. A list of food substitutes should help if you run out of an ingredient at an inopportune time. Convection Oven Cooking, High Altitude Cooking and Meal Planning and Shopping Tips sections offer special help.

In the back of the book is an ingredient index referencing recipes that could help use leftover ingredients.

I hope you find this unique cookbook helpful in setting up and enjoying your limited kitchen or galley workspace.

Susan Maza

How To Get The Most Out Of Your Basic Kitchen Utensils

The following is a list of utensils and suggestions of how I use them. Kitchen or galley space is very precious. Come up with at least two ways of using each utensil before including it in your kitchen. Then you will have the space to store those few items you just can't live without. This is just a suggested list with which two people can comfortably live. Your list may include a few different items (e.g., I don't take a mixer or eggbeater because the only thing I have not been able to do is beat egg whites, which I seldom do).

4-qt. Dutch oven with lid-great for frying because splatters are contained, proof box for yeast dough

8-inch nonstick fry pan-eggs and sauté vegetables

10-inch nonstick fry pan-top-of-the-range entrees, cooking pizza on the range top

2-qt. nonstick saucepan-vegetables, pastas, rice, hot cereals

1½-qt. heavy saucepan-sauces, mashed potatoes

2 – plastic, translucent flour and sugar canisters (rectangular-shaped are best for storage space)

2-cup glass measure

1-cup glass measure

8 x 8-inch baking dish-casseroles and baked goods for a larger group, marinating chicken breasts

large stainless steel mixing bowl

medium stainless steel mixing bowl

small stainless steel mixing bowl

hand citrus juicer for juicing citrus fruits

9-inch round cake pan-single layer cakes, brownies, as a tray for hamburger condiments or veggies

9-inch round pie plate-pies, heat rolls

½-cup glass serving dish-serving dish for salad dressings, nuts, dips and spreads for crackers or veggies, use as a container for floating a flower or two on the kitchen or picnic table

2cup glass or ceramic casserole or souffle dish-two serving casserole recipes, salsa to go with chips, two serving dessert recipes, pie plate for two

1 ½-qt. casserole dish-four serving casserole or main dish recipes

1 – 2 resealable plastic microwave oven containers-food storage and reheating

Kitchen Utensils, Cont'd.

4 or 5 glass or plastic containers of assorted sizes-food storage

2-qt. rectangular, plastic container with snap-close pour spout for juices, punches and iced tea

4-qt. rectangular, aluminum slow cooker with nonstick finish-soups, spaghetti sauce, chili, baked beans, stew, pot roast (I like this type because the pan can be used to brown or sauté foods before heating in the crock pot with no additional additional pans required. And it's easy to clean.)

11-inch square, nonstick, griddle-grilled sandwiches, French toast, pancakes

12-inch nonstick, heavy, round pizza/cookie pan-place under dishes baking in the oven to catch spills and splatters, baking cookies, oven-baked pizza

7 x 11-inch nonstick, heavy baking pan-casseroles for six people,

9 x 13-inch nonstick, heavy baking pan-baking a cake for a crowd, use as a tray to set a picnic table (things won't roll off), marinating flank steak

empty wine bottle-rolling pin, potato masher, crush crackers for toppings, make cookie crumbs for pie crusts

blender-whipping cream, homemade salad dressings, slushy drinks

4 cup coffee maker

6 – plastic shoe storage boxes with lids that nest underneath the open box. One for each of the following:
- spices
- oils, baking supplies
- vinegars, vanilla, Worcestershire sauce
- dry mixes, gelatin
- pastas
- coffee cups , wine glasses

medium-sized, rectangular, plastic cutting board-easier to store than a round one and lighter weight than wood

12-inch tongs-barbecues, serving salads

wire whisk (beating egg whites, stirring sauces and gravies)

large carving knife-cutting whole chickens, meats

medium carving knife-fruits and vegetables

2 – paring knives-cutting fruits and trimming vegetables

serrated knife-cutting breads, tomatoes

small spreader-spreading mayonnaise, spreads on crackers, frosting a cake

4 steak knives

hand potato peeler

meat thermometer-to make sure your barbequed and roasted meats are cooked thoroughly

ice cream scoop-one with liquid in the handle works best

Kitchen Utensils, Cont'd.

refrigerator thermometer (because small refrigerators should be
  monitored)
oven thermometer
garlic press
chip clips (or clothes pins) and "twisties" (close plastic bags to keep
  foods fresh)
flat food grater (much easier to store than a square one)
butane gas lighter and matches (lighting oven, range burners, candles,
  camp fires)
small knife sharpener or whetstone and oil
wine bottle opener
bottle/can opener (church key)
hand can opener
measuring spoons
metal and plastic/nylon pancake turners
plastic/nylon cooking spoon-for nonstick pans
small and large rubber scrapers-cleaning bowls, jars
10-inch meat fork-baking potatoes, barbeques, roasts
2 sets of dish clothes, hand towels and dish drying towels
3 heavy potholders
4 place settings of lightweight plates, salad plates, bowls, coffee cups
food wraps (foil, plastic wrap and resealable bags of varing sizes)
8 place settings of eating utensils – knives, forks, teaspoon and
  tablespoons (salad forks not necessary)
3 – 4 serving/mixing spoons
grapefruit knife or spoons
plastic flatware storage tray with five compartments
4 double wall, insulated plastic cups-to keep drinks cold
4 stemless glasses for wine (this will reduce the breakage of glassware)
2 insulated travel mugs-for automobile or cockpit use
rectangular, plastic table cloth and clips
toothpicks
dish soap
hand soap
paper towels
napkins and holder-to prevent loosing napkins if breezy
salt and pepper shakers-best if they have closable caps
garbage bags for garbage and use for transporting laundry

Food Staples

This list of food staples will assist in determining what foods you should always have on hand from which you can create a number of dishes if you are caught in a pinch.

Perishables
milk
buttermilk
bread
eggs
cheese (cottage, cheddar, cream, mozzarella, etc.)
butter/margarine
vegetables (including lettuce)
fruits
juices
meats, fish and poultry
plain &/or flavored yogurt

Canned Goods
beans (baked and other)
corn
tuna, salmon & crab
cream of mushroom & cream of chicken soup
concentrates

Canned Goods, cont'd.
tomatoes
tomato paste & sauce
spaghetti sauce
fruits
evaporated & sweetened, condensed milk
chicken and beef stock

Dry Goods
beverages: coffee, tea, pop, beer, liquor, wine
syrup (maple, corn, etc.)
honey
peanut butter
jam/jelly
breakfast cereals (hot and cold)
flour and corn meal

Dry Goods cont'd.

sugar (white, powdered and brown)
cooking oils (vegetable, olive, sesame, etc.)
food release spray
yeast (dry fast-acting)
baking cocoa &/or baking chocolate
baking powder and baking soda
cornstarch
vanilla
chocolate chips
spices (including salt and pepper) and herbs
vinegars (red wine, white, cider, rice, balsamic)
Liquid Smoke
condiments (mustard, mayonnaise, ketchup, horseradish,
        Worcestershire sauce)
salsa
soy sauce
salad dressing/mixes
snack foods (potato chips, crackers)
dried fruits (raisins, prunes, apples, etc.)
rice and pasta
dried lentils, peas, beans
nuts
gelatins (flavored and plain)

Emergency Food Substitutions

If You Don't Have:	Substitute:
1 c. cake flour	1 c. less 2 T. all-purpose flour
1 T. cornstarch for thickening	2 T. all-purpose flour
1 tsp. baking powder	¼ tsp. baking soda + ½ c. buttermilk or sour milk (and delete ½ c. liquid called for in the recipe)
	or
	¼ tsp. baking soda + ½ tsp. cream of tartar
1 c. corn syrup	1 c. granulated sugar + ¼ c. water
1-oz. (square) chocolate	3 T. baking cocoa + 1 T. margarine
1 c. honey	1 ¼ c. granulated sugar + ¼ c. water
1 c. brown sugar	¼ c. molasses + 1 c. granulated sugar
1 c. granulated sugar	1 c. packed brown sugar
	or
	2 c. sifted powdered sugar
1 c. powdered sugar	1 c. granulated sugar + 1 tsp. cornstarch
1 c. tomato juice	1/2 c. tomato sauce + ½ c. water
1 c. tomato sauce	1/4 c. + 2 T. tomato paste + ½ c. water
1 tsp. dry mustard	1 T. prepared mustard
1 c. light cream	2 T. butter + 1 shy c. milk
1 c. sour milk or buttermilk	1 T. lemon juice or vinegar + enough sweet milk to make 1 c. (let stand 5 min.)
	or
	reconstituted powdered buttermilk
	or
	2/3 c. plain yogurt + 5 ½ T. water
ricotta cheese	cottage cheese
1 c. whole milk	2/3 c. evaporated milk + 1/3 c. water
	or
	1 c. reconstituted nonfat dry milk + 2 T. butter
sour cream	plain yogurt

Convection Oven Cooking

Both convection and radiant ovens heat the oven cavity with radiant coils. The difference is the air in a convection oven is kept in constant motion by a fan. Circulation of hot air disrupts the natural cold barrier around the food. The result is faster and more even cooking because of the constant heat surrounding the food. Other benefits include less hot air in the kitchen or galley, less energy used saves money, and quicker recovery time results in less temperature fluctuation in the oven.

Small domestic convection ovens can be tricky. They aren't as accurate in temperature as full-size convection ovens. An oven thermometer can save aggravation and frustration. It allows you to calibrate your oven so you will know the exact oven temperature.

Choosing the proper pans can increase your success. For cookies and cakes choose shiny, bright pans. Breads and pies do better in dark or dull pans. Darker pans absorb heat and give the darker browning surface desired. The newer silicone pans work well. Lower sides on casserole dishes and roasting pans allow cold food to heat more evenly and rapidly with circulating air. Stay away from casseroles with lids and high-sided pans because they block the heat from circulating evenly around the food and therefore causing inefficiency. Baked goods with thick crusts (such as breads and pies) and roasts turn out better than cookies and deep roasting dishes. Lighter pastries and meringues may set at a tilt due to the circulating air currents.

Success Tip: Convection oven fans move hot air around which helps speed cooking. To counter this it is commonly recommended to lower the oven temperature by 25 - 30 degrees F (1 to 4 degrees C) or reduce the cooking time by 25 percent. Start checking for doneness 5 – 10 minutes before the expected finish time. Keep in mind the average temperature lost when checking the doneness of a food cooking in an oven is 50 degrees F (10 degrees C).

High Altitude Cooking

Altitudes over 3000 feet (914 meters) may require special food preparation techniques, temperature adjustments and ingredient portion changes. Having knowledge of high altitude cooking principles will help you understand what should be done to produce a quality finished food product. It may also help you resolve a cooking problem.

Due to decreased atmospheric pressure at high altitudes:

• Water boils at lower temperatures the higher you go. For example: water boils at 212 degrees F (100 degrees C) at sea level, 203 degrees F (95 degrees C) at 5000 feet (1524 meters) and 198 degrees F (92 degrees C) at 7500 feet (2286 meters). As a result a three-minute egg will take longer to cook the higher you go.

• Liquids evaporate faster at higher altitudes. Baked goods could be dry because moisture molecules escape. Adjust the recipe to include more liquid in your recipes.

Because of this additional evaporation, concentration of sugar and fat increases rapidly rather than gradually. This will decrease batters and doughs ability to trap and hold air during proofing (rising) and baking resulting in collapsing baked products. Also, sugars will cause foods to stick to pans, so grease pans generously.

• Leavening gasses in baked goods expand more so baked goods will rise faster. It is important to reduce amounts of baking powder and baking soda. Otherwise, air cells in batters will expand and rupture resulting in a coarse texture (soufflés and cheesecakes are good examples of this).

Tips and Suggestions:

• Allow for slightly decreased cooking time the higher the elevation.

• Decrease baking time by 5 minutes or more.

• Read the special directions on packages for high altitude cooking.

- Above 5000 ft (1524 meters), cooked puddings and cream pie filling temperatures don't rise high enough for maximum gelatinization of starch. Therefore, use direct heat instead of a double boiler.

- Don't over beat eggs or too much air will be incorporated in the batter or dough. Egg whites should be beaten only to the soft peak stage.

- Increase oven temperature except when baking chocolate or delicate cakes (because they may burn).

- Cookie recipes may need only minor adjustments such as slightly increased baking temperature, and/or decreasing baking powder or soda, fat and sugar, and/or increasing liquid and flour.

- At 7500 ft. (2286 meters) decrease fat by 10%.

- Reduce the proofing time in yeast doughs so they don't rise too much and collapse. Even using a "quick rising" dry yeast may require punching down before forming into loaves, braids or rolls so flavor and cell structure can develop. Standard yeast doughs may need a second proofing time. Don't go by time when proofing. You can tell visually when the dough is doubled in size.

- Increasing the size or amount of eggs in a recipe can also add strength to the weak cell structure.

- Only repeated experiments with recipes will give you more successful results. Keep good notes on page along side your recipe.

Adjustment	3000 ft. (914 m.)	5000 ft. (1524 m.)	7500 ft. (2286 m.)
Reduce **baking soda** by ¼ of amount called for except when being used to neutralize acidic liquids, such as buttermilk			
Decrease **fats**	0	0	by ¼
For each teaspoon of **baking powder** reduce by:	1/8 tsp.	1/8-1/4 tsp.	1/4 tsp.
For each cup **sugar** reduce by:	0-1 Tbl.	0-2 Tbl.	1-3 Tbl.
For each cup **liquid** increase by:	1-2 Tbl.	2-4 Tbl.	3-4 Tbl.
Increase **baking temperature** by:	15 degrees F (9 degrees C)	20 degrees F (7 degrees C)	25 degrees F (4 degrees C)

Meal Planning and Shopping Tips

• Before preparing a shopping list write down all the perishable and frozen foods and leftovers you want to use. This helps you visualize grouping things to create menus.

• Plan a full week of meals at one time leaving room for flexibility. Sometimes you may not be around for lunch or have someone over for appetizers before dinner.

• When menu planning use leftovers and perishable foods that are about to go bad first.

• Try to go to the grocery store once a week. No need to waste valuable time and gas when on vacation. This could be especially helpful when you are dry camping or a long way from a store.

• Store leftovers in freezer containers or sealed bags with a label noting the contents, date and quantity. A piece of masking tape can be marked with a ballpoint pen. Place the label on a dry surface of the container (example: "tuna casserole for one - 9/22").

• Keep a running shopping list so when you run out of something you will be sure to get it the next time you are at a store. When you use up something, write it down.

• Make a computer generated or handwritten shopping list of all the food items you want to have on hand. Tape it to the inside of your pantry door where you can note things as you run low on an item. Then it is ready to go when you are.

• Keep lists of you favorite stores with locations (e.g. Costco, Trader Joe's, Sam's Club, etc.) so you can plan on shopping there when in the area. Most of these places have the lists available upon request.

Table of Contents

Appetizers & Beverages

Favorite Recipes

_____

_____

_____

_____

_____

_____

_____

_____

_____

_____

_____

_____

_____

Helpful Hints

- You won't need sugar with your tea if you drink jasmine tea or any of the lighter-bodied varieties, like Formosa Oolong, which have their own natural sweetness. They are fine for sugarless iced tea, too.

- Calorie-free club soda adds sparkle to iced fruit juices, makes them go further and reduces calories per portion.

- For tea flavoring, dissolve old-fashioned lemon drops or hard mint candy in your tea. They melt quickly and keep the tea brisk!

- Most diets call for 8 ounces of milk and 4 ounces of fruit juice. Check your glassware. Having the exact size glass ensures the correct serving amount.

- Make your own spiced tea or cider. Place orange peels, whole cloves, and cinnamon sticks in a 6-inch square piece of cheesecloth. Gather the corners and tie with a string. Steep in hot cider or tea for 10 minutes or longer if you want a stronger flavor.

- Always chill juices or sodas before adding to beverage recipes.

- To cool your punch, float an ice ring made from the punch rather than using ice cubes. Not only is this more decorative, but it also inhibits melting and diluting.

- Place fresh or dried mint in the bottom of a cup of hot chocolate for a cool and refreshing taste.

- One lemon yields about ¼ cup juice; one orange yields about ⅓ cup juice. This is helpful in making fresh orange juice or lemonade!

- Never boil coffee; it brings out the acid and causes a bitter taste. Store ground coffee in the refrigerator or freezer to keep it fresh.

- Always use COLD water for electric drip coffee makers. Use 1 to 2 tablespoons ground coffee for each cup of water.

- Seeds and nuts, both shelled and unshelled, keep best and longest when stored in the freezer. Unshelled nuts crack more easily when frozen. Nuts and seeds can be used directly from the freezer.

- Cheeses should be served at room temperature, approximately 70°.

- To prevent cheese from sticking to a grater, spray the grater with cooking spray before beginning.

Appetizers & Beverages

SALSA & CREAM CHEESE DIP

⅓ c. salsa
3-oz. pkg. cream cheese, softened

1 small garlic clove, pressed

Mix salsa, cream cheese with garlic. This is excellent for dipping tortilla chips and vegetables. It is also good as a spread on meat sandwiches. Makes about ⅔ c.

HOT ARTICHOKE SPREAD

4 oz. cream cheese, softened
half of 14-oz. can water packed
   artichoke hearts
2 T. mayonnaise

3 T. sour cream
⅓ c. grated Parmesan cheese
1 clove garlic
¼ tsp. dill weed

Preheat oven to 350°. Combine cream cheese, drained and chopped artichoke hearts, mayonnaise, sour cream, Parmesan cheese, garlic and dill in a medium bowl. Pour mixture into a greased 1-qt. casserole dish or 9x5x3-inch loaf pan. Bake for 30 minutes until bubbly and slightly golden on top. Serve with vegetable sticks or crackers. Makes about 1½ cups.

FABULOUS BLUE CHEESE SPREAD

4 oz. cream cheese, softened
4 T. (half cube) margarine,
   softened
2 oz. crumbled blue cheese

15 black olives, chopped
1 T. Worcestershire sauce
3 T. walnuts or pecans, chopped

Mix cream cheese, margarine, blue cheese, olives, Worcestershire sauce and nuts in a small bowl. Serve with variety crackers or on toasted French bread. Makes about 1½ cups.

1

SKINNY GREEK BEAN SPREAD

16-oz. can garbanzo beans   1½ tsp. sesame oil
⅓ c. fresh lemon juice   2 to 3 dashes hot sauce
2 cloves garlic

Put garbanzo beans, lemon juice, garlic, sesame oil and hot sauce in blender. Blend well. Occassionally scrape down sides of blender. Serve with crackers, toasted bread or toasted pita bread. Makes about 2 cups.

BARBECUED MIXED NUTS

1 T. margarine   dash of hot sauce
2 T. Worcestershire sauce   2 c. salted, mixed nuts
1½ tsp. ketchup

Preheat oven to 400°. Melt margarine in medium saucepan. Mix in ketchup, hot sauce and nuts. Stir to coat nuts evenly. Spread on foil lined baking pan. Toast in oven for 15 minutes. Turn out onto paper towels to absorb excess fat. Makes about 2 cups.

ZINGY CUCUMBER CHIPS

½ c. sugar   about ⅓ c. water
about ½ c. cider vinegar   1 sm. peeled, sliced cucumber

Measure sugar in 2-cup measuring cup. Add enough vinegar to fill to ⅔ c. mark. Then add enough water to fill to 1 c. mark. Stir until sugar is dissolved. Pour brine over prepared cucumbers in a glass dish or jar. Marinate overnight in refrigerator.

60736D-02

SMOKED SALMON CHEESE SPREAD

6-oz. can boneless, skinless
  salmon, drained
4 oz. cream cheese, softened
2 T. green onions, finely chopped
4 drops Liquid Smoke

¼ c. walnuts or pecans, chopped
1½ tsp. fresh lemon juice
½ tsp. prepared, grated
  horseradish

Mix salmon, cream cheese, green onion, Liquid Smoke, nuts, lemon juice and prepared horseradish in bowl. Serve with crackers. Makes 1½ cups.

CRAB MEAT SPREAD

3-oz. pkg. cream cheese, softened
1½ tsp. grated onion
1 tsp. fresh lemon juice

¼ tsp. Worcestershire sauce
¼ c. + 2 T. sour cream
7-oz. can crab meat, drained

Mix cream cheese, onion, lemon juice, Worcestershire sauce, sour cream and crab meat in medium bowl. Serve with crackers or toasted slices of French bread. Makes about 1¾ cups.

PINK FRUIT FRAPPE

1 c. chilled cranberry juice
  cocktail
1 c. chilled apple juice
1 small, ripe banana, peeled and
  cut into chunks

¼ c. sugar
2 T. chilled milk
1½ tsp. fresh lemon juice
4 ice cubes

Combine cranberry juice, apple juice, banana chunks, sugar, milk and lemon juice in blender. Process until smooth. Add ice cubes and process until frothy. Pour into chilled glasses. Makes 3 servings.

60736D-02

HOT BUTTERED RUM BATTER

1 cube butter, softened   ¼ tsp. nutmeg
⅔ c. brown sugar   ⅛ tsp. ground cloves
¾ tsp. ground cinnamon

Thoroughly mix butter, brown sugar, cinnamon, nutmeg and cloves together. Store batter in refrigerator or freezer in a sealed container. To serve: stir 1 heaping teaspoon into 8 oz. cup of boiling water until dissolved. Add 1 oz. dark rum. Makes approx. 1 cup of batter.

KILLER MARGARITAS

1 oz. dark tequila   ½ oz. triple sec
1 oz. Rose's Sweetened Lime
Juice

For a margarita on the rocks, put several ice cubes in a glass and add tequila, sweetened lime juice and triple sec and stir. For blended margaritas, put the same ingredients with a couple of ice cubes into a blender and blend. Serves 1.

FRUIT JUICE OR WINE COOLER

½ c. any cranberry juice or   ⅔ c. seltzer water
cranberry juice blend   2 slices lime
½ c. orange juice   2 slices orange
½ c. Merlot, dry red wine or grape
juice

Combine cranberry juice, orange juice, wine or grape juice and seltzer water in a pitcher. Serve over ice cubes and garnish with lime and orange slices. Makes about 2 cups.

60736D-02

GREEK OLIVE & GARLIC SPREAD

¾ c. pitted Greek or Kalamata   1 medium garlic clove
olives   2 T. virgin olive oil

Blend olives, garlic and olive oil in blender until puréed. Serve as an appetizer spread on toasted slices of French bread or warmed slices of a baguette. Makes ¾ cup.

COCKTAIL SAUCE FOR SHRIMP OR CRAB

¼ c. ketchup   1½ tsp. fresh lemon juice
½ tsp. prepared, grated
horseradish

Mix together ketchup, horseradish and lemon juice. Makes ⅓ c.

EASY CHUTNEY CHEESE BALL

8-oz. pkg. cream cheese, softened   ¼ c. pecans or walnuts, chopped
⅓ bottle Major Gray's mango
chutney

In a small bowl mix together cream cheese with chutney using an electric mixer. Chill and form into a ball. Roll in chopped nuts. If you don't want to form a cheese ball put mixture in a serving dish and serve with a spreader.

60736D-02

BACON-CHEESE SPREAD WITH CHUTNEY OR BERRY PRESERVES

1-2 slices bacon, fried and
   drained
1½ c. shredded cheddar @ room
   temperature
1 green onion top, sliced
2 T. mayonnaise

heavy pinch of cayenne
1½ T. walnuts or pecans,
   chopped
4 T. berry (or other tart) preserves
   or chutney

Crumble bacon into medium bowl. Add cheese, onion, mayonnaise, cayenne and nuts and mix together. Scoop into a serving bowl, cover and refrigerate a few hours before serving. Serve with the preserves and an assortment of crackers on the side. Makes about 1½ c.

RECIPE FAVORITES

60736D-02

S

Soups & Salads

Favorite Recipes

_____
_____
_____
_____
_____
_____
_____
_____
_____
_____
_____
_____
_____

Helpful Hints

- Fresh lemon juice will remove onion scent from hands.

- To save money, pour all leftover vegetables and water in which they are cooked into a freezer container. When full, add tomato juice and seasoning to create a "free" soup.

- Instant potatoes are a good stew thickener.

- Three large stalks of celery, chopped and added to about two cups of beans (navy, brown, pinto, etc.), will make them easier to digest.

- When cooking vegetables that grow above ground, the rule of thumb is to boil them without a cover.

- A lump of sugar added to water when cooking greens helps vegetables retain their fresh color.

- Never soak vegetables after slicing; they will lose much of their nutritional value.

- Fresh vegetables require little seasoning or cooking. If the vegetable is old, dress it up with sauces or seasoning.

- To cut down on odors when cooking cabbage, cauliflower, etc..., add a little vinegar to the cooking water.

- To avoid tears when cutting onions, try cutting them under cold running water or briefly placing them in the freezer before cutting.

- Perk up soggy lettuce by soaking it in a mixture of lemon juice and cold water.

- Vinegar can remove spots caused by tomatoes. Soak the spot with vinegar and wash as usual.

- Egg shells can be easily removed from hard-boiled eggs if they are quickly rinsed in cold water after they are boiled. Also, add a drop of food coloring to help tell the cooked eggs apart from the raw ones in your refrigerator.

- Keep bean sprouts and jicama fresh and crisp up to five days by submerging them in a container of water, then refrigerating them.

- Your fruit salads will look perfect when you use an egg slicer to make perfect slices of strawberries, kiwis, or bananas.

Soups & Salads

SPLIT PEA SOUP

half of 16-oz. bag dry split peas
4 c. water
1 celery stalk
1 medium carrot, cut into 1-inch
   chunks
1 clove garlic

½ medium onion
8 oz. cooked smoked or link
   sausage, chopped
½ tsp. salt
⅛ tsp. pepper

Rinse and sort out rocks from dry peas. Place cleaned split peas in crock pot with 2½ c. water. Put remaining 1½ c. water, celery stalk, carrot chunks, garlic and onion into blender. Turn on blender to medium speed and almost purée the vegetables. Pour into the crock pot. Add sausage, salt and pepper. Using medium setting cook for 6 hours. Serves 5.

MINESTRONE SOUP

3 slices bacon, finely chopped
1 c. chopped onion
½ c. chopped celery
2 large cloves garlic, pressed
1 tsp. basil
10½-oz. can beef stock
11½ -oz. can bean with bacon
   soup concentrate

1½ soup cans of water
16-oz. can chopped tomatoes
½ c. macaroni
salt and pepper
1 c. cabbage, cut into thin shreds
1 c. zucchini, cubed
¾ tsp. chili powder
Parmesan cheese

In large saucepan start browning bacon. When half cooked add onion, celery, garlic and basil. Cook until tender. Stir in beef stock, canned soup, water, tomatoes, macaroni, salt, pepper and chili powder. Bring to a boil. Cover and reduce heat to low so soup can simmer for 15 minutes. Add cabbage and zucchini. Cook 12 minutes, stirring occasionally. When serving top with Parmesan cheese. Makes 2 quarts.

60736D-02

MY FRENCH ONION SOUP

1 large onion, sliced
¼ c. margarine
1 T. flour
½ c. dry red wine
1 c. chicken stock
1 c. beef stock
half of 10½-oz. can consume
   soup concentrate

⅛ tsp. dry mustard
¼ tsp. worcestershire sauce
¼ c. dry vermouth
toasted slices of French bread
shredded Gruyere or Swiss
   cheese

Sauté onion and margarine in large saucepan. When golden brown, add flour and stir until flour is well blended into the margarine. Add wine, chicken stock, beef stock, consume, dry mustard, worcestershire sauce and vermouth. Stir to blend ingredients and simmer for 30 minutes. Toast slices of French bread and place half a slice in the bottom of each soup bowl before spooning cooked soup on top. Top with cheese and serve. If you prefer to melt cheese, place bowls in microwave oven and heat for several seconds per bowl. Makes 5½ cups.

LENTIL SOUP

4 oz. Jimmy Dean regular sausage
⅔ c. chopped onion
¾ c. lentils
3 c. water
2-3 T. chopped, cooked ham

¼ tsp. coriander
½ tsp. fresh grated ginger
salt and pepper
1-1½ T. fresh lemon juice
sour cream

In a large saucepan brown sausage, breaking up the sausage with the back of a spoon as it is cooking. Once the sausage is broken up add the onion and cook with the sausage until onion is clear. Put into a crock pot along with the lentils, water, ham, coriander, ginger, salt, pepper and lemon juice. Stir. Cover and cook for 6-8 hours. Top with sour cream when serving. Makes about 1 quart.

60736D-02

FISH GUMBO

2-3 strips of bacon, chopped
flour
¼ c. chopped onion
¼ c. chopped celery
¼ c. diced red pepper
1 small garlic clove, pressed
⅛ tsp. thyme
⅛ tsp. oregano

⅛ tsp. pepper
pinch of cayenne
14½-oz. can chicken stock
4 oz. smoked sausage, cut into
   bite-size pieces
¼-½ lb. raw fish of your choice,
   cut into 1-inch cubes

In medium saucepan cook bacon until done. Remove and drain on a paper towel. Heat bacon drippings just to smoking point. Add enough flour to make a thick paste consistency. Heat until flour turns the color of a brown paper bag. Add onion, celery, red pepper, garlic, thyme, oregano, pepper, cayenne and chicken stock. Simmer for 15 minutes, stirring to prevent sticking. Add sausage and fish. Simmer 7 minutes or until fish is cooked. Makes about 3½ cups.

EASY BEANLESS CHILI

¾ lb. ground sirloin
¼ c. celery, chopped
¼ c. onion, chopped
10-oz. can Ro-Tel diced tomatoes
   with chilies
8-oz. can tomato sauce
½ tomato sauce can of water
1 clove garlic, pressed

½ tsp. oregano
1 tsp. cumin
1 T. chili powder
salt and pepper
½ of 15-oz. can of red kidney
   beans, drained and rinsed
   (optional)

In medium saucepan brown meat with onions and celery, breaking up chunks of the beef with the back of a spoon. Put all ingredients in a crock pot and cook on medium temperature for 6-8 hours. Makes about 4 cups.

60736D-02

BLACK BEAN SOUP

2 14-oz. cans black beans
14½-oz. can chicken stock
1 tsp. cumin
½ tsp. coriander
3 T. fresh lime juice

¼ tsp. red pepper flakes
salt and pepper
sour cream
1 c. cucumber, diced
3 T. onion, diced

Drain and rinse beans. In blender, blend ⅔ of the beans, chicken stock, cumin, coriander, lime juice, red pepper flakes, salt and pepper. Pour into a medium saucepan. Add the remaining beans and heat to simmering. Simmer 15 minutes stirring occasionally. Serve with a dollop of sour cream, cucumber and onion on top. Serves 3.

LEMON-CHICKEN SOUP

chicken breast half, boneless,
   skinless
¾ c. water
⅓ c. raw rice
1 T. margarine
1 T. flour
¼ c. onion, chopped
half stalk celery, diced
1 medium carrot, peeled and
   grated

3 c. chicken stock
½ c. whipping cream
1 egg, beaten well
2 T. fresh lemon juice
1½ tsp. fresh dill, finely chopped
½ tsp. lemon zest
salt and pepper

In small saucepan simmer chicken in water for 15 minutes until cooked through. Remove chicken and cool slightly before dicing or shredding. Into the water pour the rice and cover. Bring to a boil and then reduce heat. Simmer for 20 minutes. In the meantime, make a roux by melting margarine and add flour. Stir to combine. In a medium saucepan cook the onion, celery and carrot in stock for 10 minutes. Whisk in roux, stirring 2 minutes. Stir in cream and simmer 5 minutes. Add rice. Remove soup from the heat. To the beaten egg slowly add lemon juice and stir. Slowly add about a ladleful of soup to the egg mixture, stirring constantly. Add another ladleful and repeat by stirring. Now pour the egg mixture into the soup. Cook over medium heat, stirring until slightly thickened. Add chicken, dill, lemon zest, salt and pepper. Serves 3.

60736D-02

THAI-STYLE SHRIMP BISQUE

Marinade:

³/₄ lb. medium shrimp with shells	1¹/₂ tsp. peeled and grated fresh ginger
2 tsp. grated lime zest	³/₄ tsp. sugar
3 T. fresh lime juice	¹/₈ tsp. red pepper flakes
2 tsp. coriander	2 garlic cloves, pressed
1¹/₂ tsp. cilantro	

Peel and devein shrimp, reserving shells. Combine shrimp meat with the remaining ingredients in a resealable plastic bag. Marinate in refrigerator for 30 minutes.

Shrimp Stock:

1 c. water	reserved shrimp shells from above
2 T. dry white wine	
1¹/₂ tsp. tomato paste	

While shrimp is marinating start the stock. Combine water, wine, tomato paste and shrimp shells in a medium saucepan. Heat over medium heat until stock comes to a boil. Reduce heat and simmer for about 10 minutes until liquid is reduced to ¹/₂ cup. Strain mixture through a sieve to remove the shells. Discard shells.

Soup:

¹/₂ tsp. olive oil	2 T. flour
¹/₄ c. onion, chopped	¹/₂ c. milk
3 T. celery, chopped	1¹/₂ tsp. fresh grated lime zest
half a can of coconut milk	cilantro
1¹/₂ tsp. tomato paste	salt

In medium saucepan sauté onion and celery in olive oil until browned. Add shrimp stock, coconut milk and tomato paste, scraping to loosen browned bits. Bring to a boil. In small bowl whisk flour into milk until completely blended. Then slowly add to the bisque, stirring constantly. Reduce heat and simmer until thickened. Add shrimp and marinade. Cook 5 minutes. Stir in lime zest and cilantro. Salt to taste. Serves 3.

60736D-02

CREAM OF POTATO SOUP

2 strips bacon, chopped
¼ c. onion, chopped
¼ c. celery, chopped
2 T. green pepper, chopped

2 c. milk
1 c. mashed potatoes
salt and pepper

In a medium saucepan sauté bacon with onion, celery and green pepper over medium heat until onion is clear. Add milk, mashed potatoes, salt and pepper. Stir and simmer for 12-15 minutes. Serves 2.

SWEET GARLIC VINEGAR DRESSING

1 tsp. olive oil
1 small garlic clove, pressed
¼ c. honey

¼ c. balsamic vinegar
salt and pepper

In a 16-oz. jar with lid combine all ingredients by shaking vigorously. Good over fruit, chicken or garden greens. Makes about ½ cup.

FRAN'S FRENCH DRESSING

⅕ of small sweet onion
¼ c. sugar
¼ c. ketchup

2 T. cider vinegar
⅓ c. cooking oil
¼ tsp. paprika

Put all ingredients in blender and blend until onions are puréed. Makes about 1 cup.

HONEY MUSTARD DRESSING

¼ c. + 1 T. mayonnaise
1 T. honey
1 T. Dijon mustard
1½ T. cider vinegar

pinch of cayenne
1 small clove garlic, pressed
2 T. water

In a 16-oz. jar with lid combine all the ingredients and shake vigorously. Makes about ⅔ cup.

60736D-02

DRESSING FOR FRESH FRUIT SALAD

8-oz. cup of any fruit flavored
yogurt

1 tsp. fresh lemon or lime juice

In a medium bowl mix the yogurt and citrus juice. Toss with fresh chopped fruit.

BLUE CHEESE DRESSING

4 oz. crumbled blue or
Gorgonzola Cheese
1 tsp. fresh lemon juice
½ small garlic clove, pressed

½ c. mayonnaise
3 T. sour cream (optional)
salt and pepper
buttermilk

In a medium bowl mix together all the ingredients except the buttermilk. Thin with whatever amount of buttermilk you desire. Cover and let set in refrigerator for 3 hours before serving. Makes about ¾ cup.

LEMONY FRUIT SALAD

1 fuji or braeburn apple, peeled,
cored and diced
1 banana, peeled and sliced
1 orange, peeled, sectioned and
sections cut in half

1 c. of any other prepared fresh
fruit of your choice
2 T. fresh lemon juice

Combine all ingredients in a medium bowl and serve. Serves 4.

60736D-02

ORANGE AND RED ONION SALAD

Lemon-Basil Dressing:

1 T. fresh lemon juice	salt and pepper
1 T. olive oil	⅛ tsp. dry, chopped basil leaves

In a small jar with lid shake together all the ingredients and chill 2 hours in refrigerator before serving.

Salad:

4 lettuce leaves	1 thin slice red onion
2 peeled oranges, sliced	
crosswise	

Arrange 2 lettuce leaves on each salad plate. Fan out half the orange slices on top of each. Sprinkle the onion slices on top. Drizzle the dressing on top before serving. Serves 2.

60736D-02

ORANGE-AVOCADO SALAD

Orange Dressing:

grated zest from ½ orange
juice from 1 orange
2 T. orange juice concentrate
¼ c. cooking oil
¼ c. sugar

1½ T. red wine (or raspberry)
  vinegar
1 T. fresh lemon juice
salt and pepper to taste
½ tsp. sesame oil

In a 16-oz. jar with lid shake all the ingredients until well mixed. Chill 3 hours before serving.

Salad:

¼ head of iceberg lettuce, torn
  into bite-size pieces
⅓ peeled, sliced cucumber
1 avocado, sliced
11-oz. can chilled, drained
  mandarin oranges

4 mushrooms, sliced
1 green onion, sliced
2 T. crumbled blue cheese
sesame seeds or chopped
cashews (optional)

Place equal amounts of lettuce, cucumber, avocado, mandarin oranges and mushrooms on salad plates. Top with green onion, blue cheese and sesame seeds or cashews. Drizzle with chilled dressing before serving. Serves 2.

GREEK SALAD

2 c. shredded lettuce
1 large cooked, boneless, skinless
  chicken breast, diced
2 green onions, sliced
6 Greek or Kalamata olives
6-oz. jar of marinated artichoke
  hearts (drained with marinade
  reserved), chopped

¼ c. crumbled feta cheese
2 T. fresh lemon juice
salt and pepper

In a large bowl toss all the ingredients except the marinade. Before serving add only the bottom half of the marinade with the herbs from the marinated artichoke heart jar. Serves 2.

HOT GERMAN POTATO SALAD

Dressing:

¼ c. cider vinegar   ½ tsp. salt
1 T. sugar

In a small jar with lid shake all the ingredients until the sugar is dissolved.

Salad:

3 small russet potatoes, peeled   2 T. onion, minced
3 strips of real bacon, cooked and
  crumbled

In a medium saucepan boil potatoes until done. Immediately chop in half-inch cubes and place in medium bowl with the crumbled bacon and onion. Toss with the dressing and serve hot. Makes 3 servings.

SPINACH AND STRAWBERRY SALAD

Dressing:

2 T. sugar   ⅛ tsp. worcestershire sauce
1½ tsp. sesame oil   2 T. balsamic vinegar
2 T. olive oil   ¾ tsp. shallots or onion, minced

In a small jar with lid mix all the ingredients until sugar is dissolved.

Salad:

3 c. baby spinach, washed and   ¼ c. roasted and salted cashews,
  drained well   chopped
8 large strawberries, washed and
  quartered

Place spinach on salad plates first. Then top with strawberries and cashews. Drizzle dressing over the salad and serve. Serves 2.

60736D-02

CITRUS-CHICKEN SALAD

Dressing:

3 T. sour cream	1 tsp. fresh lemon juice
3 T. mayonnaise	1 tsp. sugar
1 tsp. grated orange zest	salt and pepper

In a small bowl mix together all the ingredients and chill for 3 hours.

Salad:

2 boneless, skinless chicken	2 green onions, sliced
breast halves	2 T. green or red pepper, diced
3 T. celery, diced	2 lettuce leaves, washed

In a medium saucepan boil chicken in 3 T. water. Cover and cook over medium heat until cooked through (about 15 minutes). Remove and discard the water or save for soups or sauces. Dice chicken in half-inch cubes and place in medium bowl with celery, onions and pepper. Chill for 1 hour or more. Toss together with dressing and serve on top of a lettuce leaf on each salad plate. Serves 2.

PEA SALAD

Dressing:

¼ c. mayonnaise	salt and pepper
¼ c. sour cream	

In a small bowl mix together all ingredients and chill.

Salad:

½ of 16-oz. package of frozen	1 green onion, sliced
peas, thawed	2 lettuce leaves
½ lb. bacon, chopped, cooked	1 tomato, cut into wedges
and drained on paper towel	2 lemon slices

In medium bowl mix together the peas, bacon, onion and dressing. Place an lettuce leaf on each salad plate. Top with the pea salad and dressing mixture. Serve tomato wedges and lemon slice on the side of each. Serves 2.

60736D-02

MY SALAD CREATION

Dressing:

2 T. water
2 T. rice vinegar
2 T. olive oil

half small garlic clove, pressed
1 T. ketchup
salt and pepper

In a small jar with lid shake all the ingredients until mixed. Chill in refrigerator until ready to serve.

Salad:

2½ c. salad greens, washed torn
into bite-size pieces
2 T. walnuts or pecans, chopped
1 pear or apple, cored and diced
in ½-inch cubes

2 T. crumbled blue cheese or
Gorgonzola cheese

On salad plates place half of the greens. Top with nuts, fruit and cheese. Drizzle with dressing. Serves 2.

TO GOOD TO PASS UP TOMATO-SHRIMP ASPIC

small package lemon gelatin
2 c. tomato (or V-8) juice
1½ tsp. vinegar
2 T. stuffed green olives, sliced
2 T. celery, chopped

2 green onions, chopped
6-oz. can shrimp, drained
lettuce leaves
mayonnaise

In 9x5x3-inch loaf pan place gelatin and boiling juice. Stir to dissolve gelatin. Add tomato (or V-8) juice, vinegar, olives, celery, onions and shrimp. Chill in refrigerator until set. Serve on a lettuce leaf and top with a dollop of mayonnaise. Serves 6-8.

60736D-02

RICE-A-RONI SALAD FOR A CROWD

6.9-oz. package chicken Rice-A
  Roni
2 T. margarine
2½ c. water
⅓ green or red pepper, diced
2 green onions, sliced

12 stuffed green olives, sliced
2 small jars marinated artichoke
  hearts and marinade, chopped
½ c. mayonnaise
1 tsp. curry

In medium saucepan combine Rice-A-Roni and margarine. Stir over medium heat while browning Rice-A-Roni. When golden brown add water, seasoning packet and cover. Simmer over low heat for 15-20 minutes. Cool before adding pepper, onion, olives, artichoke hearts, mayonnaise and curry. Stir to combine. Chill before serving. Makes 8 ½-cup servings.

TACO SALAD

½ lb. ground sirloin
2 T. onion, chopped
1 small clove garlic, pressed
½ tsp. chili powder
4 dashes hot sauce
1½ c. lettuce, broken into bite-
  size pieces

½ tomato, diced
¼ c. cheddar cheese, shredded
½ avocado, peeled and sliced
⅓ c. crumbled taco-flavored
  tortilla chips
½ of 15-oz. red kidney beans,
  drained and rinsed (optional)

In medium fry pan brown meat with onion and garlic over medium heat. While the meat is cooking place lettuce, tomato, cheese, avocado and tortilla chips in a medium bowl and toss. Serve on plates. When meat is cooked thoroughly, stir in chili powder and hot sauce. Spoon the meat mixture over the lettuce mixture. Serve with FRAN'S FRENCH DRESSING. Serves 2.

60736D-02

A FAMOUS RESTAURANT'S SALAD DRESSING

3 T. pasteurized eggs
¼ tsp. salt
pepper
1 small garlic clove, skin removed
1 T. sugar
½ tsp. dry mustard

½ tsp. basil
¼ tsp. oregano
½ tsp. worcestershire sauce
1 c. olive oil
3 T. cider vinegar
1 tsp. fresh lemon juice

In blender combine eggs, salt, pepper, garlic, sugar, mustard, basil and oregano. Add worcestershire sauce and blend. Slowly add olive oil while periodically add a little vinegar and lemon juice. Makes about 1 + cup.

BONE'S RESTAURANT CAESAR SALAD DRESSING

2 T. pasteurized eggs
1 T. Dijon mustard
1½ T. red wine vinegar
½ c. olive oil
1¼ tsp. anchovy paste

2¾ tsp. worcestershire sauce
half of a small clove garlic
½ tsp. fresh lemon juice
3 T. Parmesan or Romano cheese

Place all ingredients in a blender and blend thoroughly. I sometimes add the cheese while making the dressing instead of topping the Caesar salad with it. Makes about ¾ cup.

BROCCOLI SALAD

1½ c. broccoli florets, cut into
   bite-size pieces
2 strips bacon, cooked and
   crumbled
3 T. salted sunflower seeds

2 T. raisins
1½ tsp. onion, minced
3 T. mayonnaise
1 T. sugar
¾ tsp. cider vinegar

In medium bowl place raw broccoli, bacon, sunflower seeds, raisins and onion. Toss. In a small jar with lid place mayonnaise, sugar and vinegar. Shake to mix well. Pour into the broccoli mixture and toss. Serves 2.

60736D-02

MIX AND MATCH SALAD OR SANDWICH

Greens, Veggies and Fruits:

lettuces	pickles
arugula	avocado
spinach	apple
zucchini squash	banana
alfalfa sprouts	pear
cilantro	pineapple
bell peppers	raisins
tomato	dates
cucumber	

Breads:

sliced breads	baguette
bagel	kaiser roll
flour tortilla	English muffin
French or hoagy roll	pita or pocket bread

Proteins:

meat loaf	ham
steak	roast beef
tuna	bacon
seasoned taco meat	chicken
egg	cheeses - Gouda, cheddar, Swiss,
cooked pork roast or chops	cream, feta, Mozzarella, Asiago,
fish - salmon, halibut, cod, trout,	Gorgonzola, blue, etc.
etc.	

Spreads and Extras:

mayonnaise	SKINNY BEAN SPREAD
chutney	sunflower seeds
olive oil	chopped nuts
salad dressing	olives - stuffed green, Greek (or
meat sauces	Kalamata), black
cranberry sauce	capers
mustards & horseradish	dip
pickle relishes	

You can create a salad or sandwich if you have a combination of some of these suggested items. Use your imagination and enjoy.

60736D-02

MEXICAN CHICKEN SOUP

½ chicken, cut into pieces
1¼ c. water
10-oz. can Ro-Tel diced tomatoes
  with chilies
1 T. chili powder
½ tsp. cumin
3 T. diced onion

1 clove garlic, pressed
⅓ pkg. taco seasoning mix
¼ c. chopped black olives
½ c. cut corn
salt and pepper
2 tsp. minced cilantro

Place chicken, water, tomatoes, chili powder, cumin, onion, garlic, taco seasoning, olives, corn, salt and pepper in crock pot. Cook to a simmer for 6 hours. Remove chicken and pull meat from the bone. Skim and discard fat from the crock pot. Discard the skin and bones and return the meat to the crock pot. Serve and top with cilantro. Serves 4.

CHICKEN BISQUE

½ chicken, cut into pieces
1½ c. water
1 stalk celery
¼ c. grated carrots
1 clove garlic, pressed

1 T. diced pimento
5 T. margarine
4 T. flour
salt and pepper

In a large saucepan cook the chicken in water with celery stalk, carrots, garlic and pimento. Cover and simmer 45 minutes or until meat falls from the bones. Remove the chicken and pull meat from the bone. Discard the skin and bones. Remove the celery stalk and discard. Skim fat from the broth surface. Make roux by melting the margarine in a cup in the microwave oven and stir in the flour making a paste. Add a few tablespoons of stock to the roux and stir. Then stir the stock while you add the roux. This will thicken the soup as it continues to simmer for another 10 minutes. Add salt and pepper to taste. Serves 3-4.

60736D-02

DILL-CHICKEN SALAD

2 cooked boneless, skinless chicken breast halves, cubed	2 T. mayonnaise
	2 T. sour cream
2 T. diced celery	1/8 tsp. dill weed
hard-cooked egg, chopped	heavy pinch of dry mustard
2 T. slivered almonds	salt and pepper
2 T. cream cheese, softened	1½ c. spinach

Prepare the chicken salad the night before or a day ahead of serving. In a large bowl combine the chicken, celery, egg, almonds, cream cheese, mayonnaise, sour cream, dill, mustard, salt and pepper. Mix well, cover and refrigerate overnight. Just before serving put spinach on salad plates and scoop chicken mixture on top. Serves 2-3.

Recipe Favorites

Recipe Favorites

60736D-02

Vegetables & Side Dishes

Favorite Recipes

_____
_____
_____
_____
_____
_____
_____
_____
_____
_____
_____
_____
_____
_____

Helpful Hints

- When preparing a casserole, make an additional batch to freeze. It makes a great emergency meal when unexpected guests arrive. Just take the casserole from the freezer and bake it in the oven.

- To keep hot oil from splattering, sprinkle a little salt or flour in the pan before frying.

- Never overcook foods that are to be frozen. Foods will finish cooking when reheated. Don't refreeze cooked thawed foods.

- A few drops of lemon juice added to simmering rice will keep the grains separated.

- Green pepper may change the flavor of frozen casseroles. Clove, garlic, and pepper flavors get stronger when they are frozen, while sage, onion, and salt get milder.

- Don't freeze cooked egg whites; they become tough.

- For an easy no-mess side dish, grill vegetables along with your meat.

- When freezing foods, label each container with its contents and the date it was put into the freezer. Store at 0°. Always use frozen cooked foods within one to two months.

- Store dried pasta, rice (except brown rice), and whole grains in tightly covered containers in a cool, dry place. Always refrigerate brown rice, and refrigerate or freeze grains if they will not be used within five months.

- To dress up buttered, cooked vegetables, sprinkle them with toasted sesame seeds, toasted chopped nuts, canned french-fried onions, or slightly crushed seasoned croutons.

- Soufflé dishes are designed with straight sides to help your soufflé climb to magnificent heights. Ramekins are good for serving individual casseroles.

- A little vinegar or lemon juice added to potatoes before draining will make them extra white when mashed.

- To quickly bake potatoes, place them in boiling water for 10 to 15 minutes. Pierce their skins with a fork and bake in a preheated oven.

- To avoid toughened beans or corn, add salt midway through cooking.

Vegetables & Side Dishes

GINGER-MARMALADE YAMS

2 large yams
1 orange
⅓ c. marmalade
¼ c. orange juice

2 T. brandy
1 T. margarine, melted
¼ tsp. grated fresh ginger

Preheat oven to 325°. Grease 8x8-inch baking dish. Peel yam and cut crosswise into ¼-inch thick slices. Cut unpeeled orange crosswise in ¼-inch slices. Discard ends. In large bowl mix marmalade, orange juice, brandy, margarine and ginger. Add yams and mix to coat. Lay yam slices in overlapping layers in the bottom of the 8x8-inch baking dish. Drizzle remaining brandy mixture over the top of the yams. Cover tightly with foil. Bake in oven for 50-60 minutes. Serves 3.

CURRIED SAUCE FOR BROCCOLI OR CAULIFLOWER

one quarter of 10¾-oz. can cream
 of mushroom soup concentrate
3 T. mayonnaise
¼ tsp. curry

2 tsp. fresh lemon juice
cooked broccoli or cauliflower
 (enough for 2 servings)

Combine soup, mayonnaise, curry and lemon juice in a small bowl. Serve over cooked broccoli or cauliflower. Serves 2-3.

60736D-02

FETTUCCINI ALFREDO

1 green onion, sliced	$\frac{1}{3}$ c. whipping cream
2 T. margarine	$\frac{1}{3}$ c. sour cream
half of 14-oz. can chicken stock	$\frac{1}{3}$ c. Parmesan cheese
1$\frac{1}{2}$ tsp. vermouth or dry white wine	2 servings of cooked fettuccini or other pasta
1 egg	

Over medium heat sauté onion and margarine in medium fry pan. Add chicken stock and vermouth (or wine). In a cup beat the egg and add the whipping cream. Add the egg/cream mixture to the sautéed onion and stir while sauce thickens. Stir in sour cream and Parmesan cheese. Heat to serving temperature. Toss in the warm, cooked noodles. Serves 2.

RICE PILAF

3 T. margarine, melted	$\frac{1}{3}$ c. raw rice
$\frac{1}{2}$ c. mushrooms, chopped	half of 10$\frac{1}{2}$-oz. can consume
$\frac{1}{2}$ tsp. oregano	soup concentrate
1 green onion, sliced	$\frac{1}{2}$ c. water

Preheat oven to 450°. In a greased 1$\frac{1}{2}$-qt. casserole dish stir together all ingredients. Cover and bake for 45 minutes to 1 hour in oven. Serves 2-3.

GREEK OLIVE AND GARLIC PASTA

1$\frac{1}{2}$ c. cooked pasta (any kind)   2 T. GREEK OLIVE SPREAD

Cook and drain pasta according to directions. Add GREEK OLIVE & GARLIC SPREAD to saucepan and toss with pasta until spread is evenly dispersed. Serves 2.

60736D-02

AU GRATIN ZUCCHINI

1 T. margarine
3 medium zucchini
1 T. tarragon
¾ c. Parmesan cheese, grated

¼ c. milk
¼ c. whipping cream
1 egg

Preheat oven to 350°. Grease 1½-qt. casserole dish. Melt margarine in heavy skillet over medium heat. Add zucchini and sauté until golden (about 5 minutes). Layer half of zucchini in dish. Sprinkle with half of tarragon and ¼ c. of Parmesan cheese. Repeat layering with remaining zucchini, tarragon and ¼ c. of Parmesan. In medium bowl combine milk, cream and egg. Pour over zucchini in casserole dish. Top with remaining Parmesan cheese. Bake in oven for 30-35 minutes or until set. Serves 3.

MASHED YAMS WITH GARLIC AND GINGER

1 lb. yams, peeled and cut into
  1-inch cubes
2 T. margarine
1 medium clove garlic, pressed

2 tsp. fresh grated ginger
¼ tsp. salt
¼ c. milk

Steam yam cubes until very soft. While yams are cooking melt margarine in small saucepan. Add garlic and ginger. Heat over medium-low heat for 5 minutes. Mash yams and stir in the garlic/ginger/margarine mixture. Serves 3.

SAUTÉED YAMS WITH LEMON AND THYME

1 lb. yam, peeled and thinly sliced
2 tsp. margarine
¼ c. onion, thinly sliced
2 tsp. fresh lemon juice

2 tsp. brown sugar
large pinch of thyme
salt and pepper

In a medium fry pan melt margarine over medium heat. Add onion and sauté for 4 minutes. Add yam slices, cover and cook 10 minutes. Stir occasionally. Stir in lemon juice, brown sugar, thyme, salt and pepper. Cook covered for 5 minutes. Remove cover and continue cooking for 5 minutes, stirring occasionally. Serves 3.

60736D-02

HOLIDAY CABBAGE

half head red cabbage, cored and
   shredded or thinly sliced
2 T. olive oil
salt and pepper to taste

3 T. brown sugar
¼ c. + 2 T. dry red wine
3 T. red wine vinegar
1 T. cornstarch

Sauté cabbage in medium sauté pan with olive oil over medium heat. Cook 10 minutes. Remove from heat and add salt, pepper and brown sugar. Return to heat and stir until sugar dissolves. In a 1-cup measure combine wine, vinegar and cornstarch. Pour into cabbage mixture and mix well. Simmer 25-30 minutes. Serves 3.

RON'S BAKED BEANS

16-oz. can B&M Original Baked
   Beans
5 oz. (a little under ⅔ c.) Heinz
   Ketchup

3½ T. worcestershire sauce
3½ T. brown sugar

Preheat oven to 235°. In small mixing bowl mix all the ingredients and pour into a greased 1 to 1½-qt. casserole dish. Bake in oven for 3 hours. Serves 2-3.

STEAMED BROCCOLI WITH LEMON BUTTER

broccoli crowns or cut broccoli,
   enough for two

1-2 T. butter
2 tsp. fresh lemon juice

Steam broccoli to crisp tender. Melt butter in a cup in the microwave oven and add lemon juice. Drizzle over steamed broccoli and serve. Serves 2.

60736D-02

SCALLOPED EGGPLANT

1 small eggplant, peeled and
   diced
¼ medium onion, chopped
¼ c. milk
1 egg, beaten
2 T. margarine

⅓ c. dry bread crumbs or cracker
   crumbs
1 T. parsley, chopped
salt and pepper
⅓ c. shredded cheddar cheese (or
   another type you like)

Preheat oven to 375°. In a medium saucepan steam eggplant just until tender. In the meantime, in a small sauté pan melt 1 T. margarine and sauté the onion until golden brown. In a small bowl and using a fork blend 1 T. margarine in with the crumbs until evenly dispersed. Drain eggplant and add parsley, sautéed onion, milk/egg mixture and pour half of this into a greased 9x5x3-inch loaf pan. Sprinkle half the crumb mixture on top and a little salt and pepper. Pour remaining eggplant mixture into the loaf pan and top with the remaining crumb mixture and a little salt and pepper. Top with cheese. Bake in oven for 30 minutes. Serves 2.

GORGONZOLA AU GRATIN POTATOES

1 lb. russet potatoes, unpeeled
   and cut in half lengthwise
1 T. margarine, melted
1 tsp. dry parsley flakes
1 green onion, sliced

1 small garlic clove, pressed
salt and pepper
⅛ tsp. thyme
½ c. crumbled Gorgonzola cheese
paprika

Preheat oven to 350°. Steam potatoes until tender (about 20-25 minutes). Cool slightly and slice into ½-inch thick slices. Melt the margarine and brush around the inside of a 9x5x3-inch loaf pan. Put half the potatoes in the loaf pan, sprinkle with half of each of the following: parsley, green onion, garlic, salt, pepper, thyme and Gorgonzola cheese. Repeat the layers putting the gorgonzola on top. Sprinkle with a little paprika. Bake in oven for 20-25 minutes or until heated through. Serves 3.

60736D-02

GREAT ASPARAGUS

1 c. steamed asparagus
2 T. mayonnaise

3 T. shredded cheddar cheese

Steam asparagus until crisp tender. Discard liquid, add mayonnaise and toss. Serve and top with shredded cheddar cheese. Serves 2.

BRANDIED YAM AND POTATO AU GRATIN

1 small russet potato, peeled and cut into ⅛-inch thin slices
1 small yam, peeled and cut into ⅛-inch thin slices
salt and pepper

¼ c. chicken stock, heated
2 T. brandy
⅓ c. shredded jack (or cheddar cheese) cheese
3 T. shredded Parmesan cheese

Preheat oven to 375°. Grease a 1½-qt. casserole dish. Line the bottom of the casserole dish with an overlapping layer of alternating potato and yam slices. Sprinkle lightly with salt and pepper. Repeat layering until all yams and potatoes are used. Mix the hot chicken stock with the brandy. Pour over the potatoes. Cover dish with foil and bake in oven for about 1 hour until tender. Uncover and top with jack and Parmesan cheeses. Return to the oven and bake uncovered for 13 minutes until cheese is browned. Serves 2.

BROCCOLI AND RICE CASSEROLE

2 T. margarine
⅓ c. chopped onion, chopped
½ stalk celery, chopped
2 servings of steamed broccoli, cooked until crisp tender
half of 10¾-oz. can cream of chicken soup concentrate

½ c. shredded cheddar cheese
¾ c. cooked rice
2 dashes hot sauce
salt and pepper

Preheat oven to 350°. Grease a 1½-qt. casserole dish. Melt margarine in small sauté pan. Add onion and celery. Cook until onion is clear. In a large bowl mix together the onion mixture, steamed broccoli, chicken soup concentrate, cheese, hot sauce, salt and pepper. Pour into the casserole dish and bake in oven for 40 minutes. Serves 2-3.

60736D-02

BAKED ACORN SQUASH

1 small acorn squash	2 T. margarine
1/4 c. brown sugar	1 small apple, peeled and diced
1/4 tsp. cinnamon	rum (optional)

Poke small holes in the skin of squash with a paring knife or cooking fork. Place in 8x8-inch baking dish and cook at full power in the microwave oven for 7 minutes. Rotate and determine what additional time will be necessary to cook the squash until tender throughout (test with the knife or fork). Cut squash in half lengthwise and remove the seeds. Place the squash halves back in the baking dish with the open cavity facing up. Fill each half with 2 T. brown sugar, 1/8 tsp. cinnamon, 1 T. margarine, half of the apple and sprinkle a little rum on the top. Cover with plastic wrap and return to the microwave oven and heat until the apple is tender (about 4-5 minutes). Serves 2-3.

SPECIAL ZUCCHINI

1 strip bacon, chopped	1 zucchini, cut into 1/4-inch slices
3 T. onion, chopped	

In medium fry pan sauté the bacon over medium heat until almost done. Add onion and cook until bacon is completely cooked. Add zucchini and stir fry until tender crisp, Serve 2.

SPICED SUMMER SQUASH

1 small zucchini squash, cut into 1-inch chunks	1/4 tsp. salt
	1/4 tsp. cinnamon
1 small yellow summer squash, cut into 1-inch chunks	1/8 tsp. cumin
	1 small clove garlic, pressed
1 T. olive oil	1/4 c. raisins
3/4 tsp. curry powder	

In medium fry pan sauté the zucchini and yellow squash, olive oil, curry, salt, cinnamon, cumin, and garlic until squash is a light, golden brown in color, stirring occasionally. Add raisins and cover with a lid. Cook 3 minutes. Serves 2-3.

60736D-02

TARRAGON BUTTERED CARROTS

2 T. margarine
¼ tsp. tarragon

1½ c. baby carrots (or carrots cut into ¾-inch chunks)

In a cup melt margarine in microwave oven. Add tarragon and let the flavors marry while carrots are being prepared. Steam carrots until crisp tender. Serve and drizzle the warmed tarragon butter over carrots. Serves 2.

INDIAN SPICED RICE

1 c. water
½ c. rice
1 tsp. margarine
⅛ tsp. cinnamon

⅛ tsp. cumin
heavy pinch of turmeric
2 T. raisins

In small saucepan boil water. Stir in rice, margarine, cinnamon, cumin, turmeric and raisins. Cover and cook over low heat for 25 minutes. Serves 2.

GRILLED ZUCCHINI

3 T. olive oil
1 garlic clove, pressed
1 T. soy sauce

2 small zucchini, cut lengthwise into ½-inch strips
salt and pepper

In an 8x8-inch glass baking dish stir together olive oil, garlic and soy sauce. Add zucchini and toss to coat. Let set about 30 minutes. Place on medium hot barbecue. Cook 4 minutes per side. Season with salt and pepper. Serves 2.

60736D-02

POTATO AND SWEET ONION PACKETS

1 medium russet potato. unpeeled   4 T. margarine
  and cut into 1-inch cubes   salt and pepper
½ medium sweet onion, diced

Cut 2 12-inch lengths of foil and spray the inside with food release spray. On each piece place half the potato, half the onion, 2 T. margarine, salt and pepper. Wrap foil up around the vegetables and seal by folding the edges together. Poke about half a dozen holes in the foil with a cooking fork to allow some steam to escape while cooking. Place on barbecue and cook over a medium fire for about 45 minutes or until tender. Rotate the packets so the potatoes will cook evenly. Serves 2.

ROASTED YAMS AND POTATOES

1 small russet potato, cut into   2½ T. olive oil
  1-inch chunks   salt and pepper
1 small yam (or sweet potato), cut   ½ tsp. crushed rosemary
  into 1-inch chunks   (optional)

Preheat oven to 420°. In a medium bowl toss the potato, yam or sweet potato in olive oil. Pour potatoes onto a foil lined 8x8-inch baking dish. Sprinkle with salt, pepper and rosemary. Roast in oven for 45 minutes, turning twice while cooking to brown evenly. When tender serve. Serves 2.

ORIENTAL ASPARAGUS

½ lb. asparagus, trimmed   1 tsp. fresh lemon juice
salt   ¼ tsp. soy sauce
1 T. butter   salt and pepper
¼ tsp. sesame oil   toasted sesame seeds (optional)

Cook asparagus in medium fry pan of boiling, salted water about 5 minutes until almost crisp tender. Drain asparagus and remove from pan. Melt butter with sesame oil in the pan over medium heat. When hot return asparagus to the pan sauté until done (crisp tender). Mix in lemon juice and soy sauce. Season with salt and pepper. Serve and top with sesame seeds. Serves 2.

60736D-02

HASH BROWN AND CHEESE POTATOES

1-2 baked russet potatoes, diced
¼ c. chopped onion
2-3 T. margarine
one quarter can of cream of
   mushroom soup concentrate

¼ c. sour cream
salt and pepper
½ c. shredded cheddar cheese
paprika

Fry potatoes and onion in margarine in a medium nonstick fry pan. When light golden brown in color add the soup concentrate, sour cream, salt and pepper and stir. Top with cheese and paprika. Let cheese melt a minute or two. Serves 2.

RECIPE FAVORITES

60736D-02

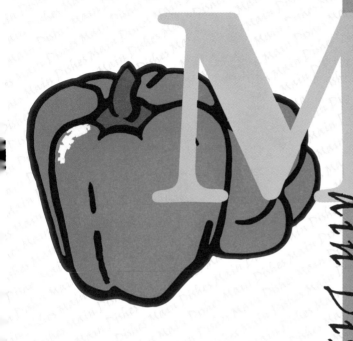

M

ain Dishes

Favorite Recipes

_____

_____

_____

_____

_____

_____

_____

_____

_____

_____

_____

_____

_____

_____

Helpful Hints

- Use little oil when preparing sauces and marinades for red meats. Fat from the meat will render out during cooking and will provide plenty of flavor. Certain meats, like ribs and pot roast, can be parboiled before grilling to reduce the fat content.

- When trying to reduce your fat intake, buy the leanest cuts you can find. Fat will show up as an opaque white coating or can also run through the meat fibers, as marbling. Although most of the fat (the white coating) can be trimmed away, there isn't much that can be done about the marbling. Stay away from well-marbled cuts of meat.

- Home from work late with no time for marinating meat? Pound meat lightly with a mallet or rolling pin, pierce with a fork, sprinkle lightly with meat tenderizer, and add marinade. Refrigerate for about 20 minutes, and you'll have succulent, tender meat.

- Marinating is a cinch if you use a plastic bag. The meat stays in the marinade and it's easy to turn and rearrange. Cleanup is easy; just toss the bag.

- It's easier to thinly slice meat if it's partially frozen.

- Tomatoes added to roasts will help to naturally tenderize them. Tomatoes contain an acid that works well to break down meats.

- Whenever possible, cut meats across the grain; they will be easier to eat and have a better appearance.

- When frying meat, sprinkle paprika over it to turn it golden brown.

- Thaw all meats in the refrigerator for maximum safety.

- Refrigerate poultry promptly after purchasing. Keep it in the coldest section of your refrigerator for up to two days. Freeze poultry for longer storage. Never leave poultry at room temperature for more than two hours.

- If you're microwaving skinned chicken, cover the baking dish with vented clear plastic wrap to keep the chicken moist.

- Lemon juice rubbed on fish before cooking will enhance the flavor and help maintain a good color.

- Scaling a fish is easier if vinegar is rubbed on the scales first.

Main Dishes

SAUSAGE CREAM PASTA

4 oz. smoked sausage, cut or
sliced into bite-size pieces
1 small garlic clove, pressed
3 T. sun dried tomatoes packed in
oil, drained and chopped (or 3
T. rehydrated, chopped, sun
dried tomatoes)

5 mushrooms, sliced
1 c. cream
1½ c. cooked pasta or rice

In large fry pan sauté sausage, garlic and tomatoes. When hot add mushrooms and cream. Reduce sauce to about ¾ c. Serve over cooked pasta or rice. Serves 2.

STROGANOFF FOR TWO

half med. onion
1 sm. clove garlic, pressed
1 T. margarine
1 beef bouillon cube
¼ c. dry red wine
2 T. ketchup
1 c. mushrooms, sliced

4 oz. cream cheese
1 c. sour cream
8 oz. cooked beef (leftover roast
is great) cut into bite-size
pieces
1½ c. cooked rice or noodles

In medium sauté pan cook onions and garlic in margarine until onions are clear. Add bouillon cube and mash with back of spoon until completely broken up. Stir in wine, ketchup and mushrooms. Heat mixture until it starts to boil. Stir to dissolve the bouillon. Add cream cheese, sour cream and beef. Heat to serving temperature. Serve over cooked rice or noodles. Serves two.

60736D-02

MEXICAN CASSEROLE

one third of 14-oz. can chicken
stock
one third of 10³/₄-oz. can cream of
chicken or cream of mushroom
soup concentrate
1 T. jalapeño peppers, chopped
¼ c. onion, chopped
½ c. black olives, chopped or
sliced

6 corn tortillas
half of 16-oz. can refried beans
1 c. cooked chicken or beef,
shredded
⅓ c. sour cream
⅔ c. shredded cheddar cheese

Preheat oven to 350°. Grease 9x5x3-inch loaf pan. In medium bowl mix the chicken stock, cream soup concentrate, peppers, onions and olives. Cut the tortillas into 2-inch strips, then in half, crosswise. In bottom of the greased pan spread one third of the soup mixture. Top with half the tortillas, half the refried beans, half the meat, half the sour cream and half the shredded cheese. Repeat the process with the top layer being the soup mixture. Bake in oven for 40-45 minutes until bubbling and golden brown on top. Serves 4.

EASY LASAGNE

2 c. spaghetti sauce (see
SPAGHETTI SAUCE WITH
MEAT)
1½ c. cooked pasta
½ c. sliced mushrooms

¼ c. black olives, sliced or
chopped
½ c. cheddar cheese, shredded
½ c. Mozzarella cheese, shredded

Preheat oven to 350°. Grease 9x5x3-inch loaf pan. In bottom of the greased pan spread one third of the spaghetti sauce. Top with half of each of the cooked pasta, mushrooms, black olives, cheddar cheese and Mozzarella cheese. Repeat the process with the top layer being the sauce. Bake in 350° oven for 35-45 minutes until top is bubbling and slightly golden brown. Serves 4.

60736D-02

SLOPPY JOES

¼ c. onion, chopped	1 T. brown sugar
¼ c. celery, chopped	1 tsp. dry mustard
2 tsp. cooking oil	2 T. lemon juice
½ lb. ground sirloin	1 tsp. Worcestershire sauce
3 T. ketchup	⅛ tsp. salt
8-oz. can tomato sauce	2-3 hamburger buns, toasted

In 10-inch fry pan sauté onion and celery in cooking oil. Add ground sirloin and break into small pieces. Cook until brown. Stir in ketchup, tomato sauce, brown sugar, mustard, lemon juice, Worcestershire sauce and salt. Simmer 20 minutes. Spoon mixture over toasted bun halves. Serves 3.

CHICKEN DIVAN

half of 10¾-oz. can cream of mushroom soup concentrate	2 boneless, skinless chicken breast halves
½ c. mayonnaise	1 pkg. frozen, chopped broccoli, thawed
¾ tsp. fresh lemon juice	½ c. cheddar cheese, shredded
⅛ tsp. curry powder	

Preheat oven to 350°. Grease a 9x5x3-inch loaf pan or 1½-qt. casserole dish. Mix the soup concentrate, mayonnaise, lemon juice and curry powder together in a 2-cup measuring cup. Spread half of the mixture on the bottom of the greased pan or dish. Place chicken breast halves on top of the sauce. Then layer the broccoli, remaining sauce and top with shredded cheese. Bake for 35-45 minutes. Serve over cooked rice. Optional cooking method including rice: for cooking in the oven add ½ c. uncooked rice and 1⅓ c. water to the soup mixture. Then finish layering the ingredients as directed above. Cook in oven 45-55 minutes. Serves 3-4.

60736D-02

KAY'S PIZZA REQUEST

Pizza Sauce:

half of 8-oz. can tomato sauce	½ tsp. oregano
half of 6-oz. can tomato paste	½ tsp. rosemary, crushed
1 tsp. sweet basil	1 clove garlic, pressed

Prepare sauce at least half a day ahead to allow for flavors to marry before assembling the pizza. In small bowl stir together tomato sauce, tomato paste, basil, oregano, rosemary and garlic. Cover bowl and refrigerate until ready to assemble pizza.

Pizza Topping Suggestions
  Include:

½ c. cooked meat (pepperoni, Canadian bacon, sausage)	¼ c. chopped onions
	2 T. chopped green peppers
¼ c. sliced olives	¼ c. chopped tomatoes
¼ c. sliced mushrooms	1½ c. various shredded cheeses
¼ c. pineapple tidbits	(at least half being Mozzarella)

The above is only a suggested list of toppings. Yours may vary. It is easiest to prepare all the toppings ahead of the dough or while dough is proofing.

Easy Pizza Crust:

half envelope of fast-acting, dry yeast	¼ tsp. salt
	⅓ c. + 1 T. warm (125°) water
1 c. flour	2 tsp. olive oil

This pizza is cooked on the range top to save on oven cleaning and eliminate the smoke that is produced during baking. To make pizza crust stir together yeast, flour and salt in a medium bowl. Add water and 1 tsp. olive oil. Stir to incorporate. Knead dough on floured surface 10 times, turning dough ¼ turn each time you knead it. Drizzle 1 tsp. olive oil into bowl. Set dough ball back into bowl and turn to evenly coat dough ball with olive oil. To proof dough, boil 2 c. water in measuring cup in microwave oven to create a steamy oven cavity. Place bowl of dough in microwave with the cup of boiled water and close door to keep dough warm and moist while proofing. You may need to remove the dough once during the proofing process to reheat the water to boiling to maintain a warm, steamy oven cavity. If you don't have a microwave oven you can proof the dough by heating 2 inches of water to 120° in a covered Dutch oven. Turn off the heat. Float the bowl of dough on the water in the covered Dutch oven. Proof until dough is
(continued)

60736D-02

doubled in size (approx. 35-45 minutes). To cook pizza preheat 11-inch, nonstick, square griddle on the lowest setting of a gas burner or medium-low on an electric burner. When evenly warmed, moisten your fingers with olive oil before handling the proofed dough. Press dough evenly over the cooking surface. Spread sauce evenly over the dough. Top with precooked meat and other preferred toppings. Sprinkle shredded cheeses on top. Loosely tent a piece foil over the top. Try to keep the cheese from touching the foil. Cook for 25-30 minutes or until crust is crispy on the bottom. Place on cutting board to cut into pieces. Makes 4 large pieces.

TUNA CASSEROLE

1½ c. uncooked pasta
6-oz. can tuna
1 small clove garlic, pressed
¼ c. onion, chopped

2 c. shredded cheddar cheese
¾ can of 10¾-oz. mushroom
 soup concentrate
⅓ c. mayonnaise

Preheat oven to 350°. Grease a 2-qt. casserole dish. In a medium saucepan boil enough water to cook pasta. While pasta is cooking mix in a large bowl the following ingredients: tuna, garlic, onion, cheese, mushroom soup concentrate and mayonnaise. Drain pasta when done. Add the drained pasta to the tuna mixture. Stir until well mixed and pour into the greased casserole dish. Bake in a 350° oven for 35 minutes. Serves 3.

60736D-02

MEDITERRANEAN CHICKEN DINNER

2 tsp. olive oil
2 boneless, skinless chicken
  breast halves
2 T. onion, chopped
1 small clove garlic, pressed
1 strip bacon, chopped
14-oz. can diced tomatoes in juice
14-oz. can chicken stock
$\frac{1}{3}$ c. dry white wine

$\frac{1}{2}$ c. water
7 pitted Greek (or Kalamata)
  olives, chopped
1$\frac{1}{2}$ tsp. thyme
1 bay leaf
$\frac{1}{2}$ tsp. basil
$\frac{1}{8}$ tsp. salt
$\frac{2}{3}$ c. dry pasta (any type)

In large nonstick fry pan brown chicken breasts on all sides in olive oil. Remove chicken and set aside. In the pan with the chicken drippings sauté onion, garlic and bacon until bacon is done. Add tomatoes and juice, chicken stock, wine, water, olives, thyme, bay leaf, basil, salt and pasta. Stir to incorporate all ingredients. Add chicken and cover pan. Cook over low heat for 30 minutes. Serves 2.

CHICKEN CACCIATORE

$\frac{1}{2}$ large onion, chopped
1 clove garlic, pressed
1 T. olive oil
$\frac{1}{2}$ chicken, cut into parts
14$\frac{1}{2}$-oz. can diced tomatoes in
  juiced
8-oz. can tomato sauce
1$\frac{1}{2}$ c. mushrooms, chopped

1 bay leaf
1 tsp. oregano
$\frac{1}{2}$ tsp. basil
$\frac{1}{4}$ tsp. rosemary
$\frac{1}{2}$ tsp. salt
$\frac{1}{8}$ tsp. pepper
$\frac{1}{4}$ c. dry white wine
1$\frac{1}{2}$ c. cooked rice

In 10-inch skillet sauté onion and garlic in olive oil. Cook until onion is clear. Remove and set aside. In the skillet brown the chicken parts. Add garlic and onion mixture, tomatoes, tomato sauce, mushrooms, bay leaf, oregano, basil, rosemary, salt, pepper and wine. Cover and simmer for 30 minutes. Serve over cooked rice. Serves 2.

60736D-02

CHICKEN-ASIAGO WITH ORZO

14-oz. can chicken stock
2 boneless, skinless chicken
 breast halves, cut into bite-size
 pieces
⅔ c. uncooked orzo (rice-shaped
 pasta)

½ c. frozen peas, thawed
⅓ c. grated Asiago cheese
pinch of salt
⅛ tsp. rosemary, basil or oregano
pinch of pepper

In medium fry pan bring chicken stock to a boil. Add chicken and orzo. Bring to a boil. Then reduce heat and simmer 12 minutes, stirring occasionally. Remove from heat and stir in peas, ¼ c. cheese, salt, herb of your choice and pepper. Serve and top with remaining cheese. Serves 2.

CHICKEN GUMBO

½ chicken
2 c. sauvignon blanc or semillon
 wine
2 c. water
1 T. Worcestershire sauce
⅛ tsp. salt

½ large onion, finely chopped
¼ c. celery, chopped
1 small clove garlic, pressed
4 T. olive oil
½ lb. smoked sausage, sliced
½ tsp. hot sauce

In a large pot boil chicken in wine, water, Worcestershire sauce and salt. Once boiling reduce heat and simmer until chicken easily falls from the bone. In the meantime, sauté onion, celery and garlic in 1 T. olive oil in a medium fry pan until onion is clear. Put mixture into pot with the simmering chicken and add sausage and hot sauce. In the fry pan add remaining olive oil and enough flour to make a thick paste. Make a roux by heating flour and oil mixture until flour becomes brown. Stir constantly. When chicken is done pull the meat in bite-size pieces from the bone and discard the bones and skin. Skim the fat from the pot and discard. Return the pulled meat to the pot with the stock mixture. Add a little stock at a time to the roux and stir to incorporate each time until the roux becomes the consistency of gravy. Then pour the roux into the pot with the chicken and stock. Heat and stir until mixture is simmering at a rolling boil. Serves 2-3.

60736D-02

SHRIMP-FETA-TOMATO PASTA

1 tsp. olive oil
1 clove garlic, pressed
pinch red pepper flakes
¼ tsp. oregano
⅛ tsp. salt
1 c. dry pasta (any type)

⅓ c. dry white wine
14-oz. can chicken stock
½ lb. peeled, deveined shrimp
¼ c. feta cheese, crumbled
1 plum tomato

In medium nonstick fry pan sauté garlic in olive oil. Add red pepper flakes, oregano, salt, dry pasta, wine and chicken stock. Cover with lid and simmer for about 10-15 minutes until pasta is tender. Add shrimp, cover pan with lid and cook 4-5 minutes. When shrimp is cooked remove lid, add feta and tomato. Toss before serving. Serves 2.

CHICKEN-ARTICHOKE HASH

2 red-skinned potatoes, cut into
  1-inch chunks
1 c. butternut squash, peeled,
  seeded and cut into 1-inch
  chunks
2 T. margarine
½ onion, chopped
2 boneless, skinless chicken
  breast halves, cut into ¾-inch
  strips

14-oz. can artichoke hearts,
  chopped
½ c. whipping cream
½ c. freshly grated Parmesan
  cheese
1 tsp. tarragon

Cook potatoes and squash in a medium saucepan with water until almost tender. Drain and discard water. In large fry pan sauté the onions in the margarine until golden brown. Add potatoes, squash, chicken and artichoke hearts and cook until slightly brown. Add cream, ⅓ c. of the Parmesan cheese and tarragon. Simmer until cream thickens and chicken is cooked. Serve and top with remaining Parmesan cheese. Serves 2-3.

60736D-02

BEEF BOURGUIGNON

2 slices bacon, coarsely chopped
¾ lb. trimmed boneless beef chuck, cubed into 1-inch chunks
salt and pepper
3 T. flour
½ onion, chopped
2 large carrots, peeled and sliced crosswise into 1-inch chunks

1 clove garlic, pressed
1 c. beef stock
2 T. brandy
1 c. dry red wine
6 mushrooms, coarsely chopped
1½ tsp. thyme
1½ tsp. brown sugar
1½ tsp. tomato paste

In large fry pan cook bacon until crisp. Remove bacon and drain on paper towel. Season beef with salt and pepper and coat with flour (using all the flour). Brown beef in bacon drippings, turning to brown on all sides. Remove beef and set aside. In pan sauté onion, carrots and garlic until onion is clear. Transfer vegetables to container holding beef. Stir in beef stock, brandy, wine, mushrooms, thyme, brown sugar and tomato paste. Boil and reduce glaze for about 8 minutes. Put all ingredients in a crock pot, cover and cook 6 hours. Serves 2.

WORLD FAMOUS RESTAURANT'S SHRIMP SPECIALTY

1 T. + 1½ tsp. olive oil
14 large prawns, peeled and deveined
2 T. butter

1 small clove garlic, pressed
2 T. dry vermouth
1 T. + 1½ tsp. fresh lemon juice
2 slices toast or 1 c. cooked rice

Pour olive oil in medium sauté pan. Heat pan to medium temperature and add shrimp and cook until slightly brown on one side. Turn, add butter and garlic. Stir until well blended and increase heat to medium-high. Add vermouth and lemon juice, stirring constantly for 1 minute. Serve over a piece of toast or rice. Serves 2.

60736D-02

SOUTHERN CHICKEN AND DUMPLINGS

½ chicken, cut into parts
1¾ c. water
2-3 stalks of celery, diced
1 tsp. salt

⅛ tsp. pepper
1 hard-cooked egg, chopped
DROP BISCUIT RECIPE

Place chicken, water, celery, salt and pepper in a large pot and cover. Bring to a boil and reduce to simmer for about 45 minutes or until chicken meat falls from the bone. In the meantime, boil the egg in water for 10 minutes. Place in cold water 10 minutes before peeling. Dice peeled egg and set aside. When the chicken is done remove the meat and skin from the bone. Discard the skin and bones. Skim fat from the broth surface and discard. Break the meat into bite-size pieces and return to the broth with the diced egg. Make DROP BISCUIT RECIPE except after stirring all ingredients together gather all the dough in your hands and press into a ball. Place on a lightly floured surface and knead 4 times. Roll or pat dough ball until it is about ¼-inch thick. Cut into 1-inch strips that are no longer than 3 inches in length. Bring broth and chicken to a rolling boil and place strips of the biscuit dough on the top of the broth in a single layer. Leaving lid off simmer for 10 minutes. Put lid on pot and simmer another 10 minutes. Serves 2.

ROBIN'S FAVORITE

1 T. olive oil
¼ c. onion, chopped
½ of small garlic clove, pressed
14½-oz. can diced tomatoes in juice
½ tsp. basil
⅛ tsp. red pepper flakes
1 c. chicken stock

¾ c. dry pasta
½ c. packed grated Havarti cheese
7 Kalamata or Greek olives, chopped or sliced
2 T. freshly grated Parmesan cheese

In large saucepan sauté onion and garlic in olive oil over medium heat until onion is clear. Add tomatoes and juice, basil. red pepper flakes and chicken stock. Bring to a boil and reduce heat so mixture simmers uncovered for 45 minutes. Add dry pasta and simmer for 20 to 25 minutes until pasta is tender but still firm. Enough sauce liquid should be absorbed by the pasta but still leave a thickened tomato sauce. Add more chicken stock or water if necessary. Stir in Havarti cheese and Kalamata olives. Top with Parmesan cheese. Serves 2.

60736D-02

SALMON WITH LIME-THYME MAYONNAISE

2 T. pasteurized egg
1 tsp. Dijon mustard
¼ tsp. grated lime peel
½ c. olive oil
1 T. fresh lime juice

⅛ tsp. salt
⅛ tsp. thyme
2 servings of barbecued or baked salmon

Put egg, mustard, lime peel and ¼ c. olive oil in blender and blend on medium. Slowly add lime juice. When that is incorporated add the remaining ¼ c. olive oil, salt and thyme. Serve over barbecued or baked salmon. Serves 2.

BAKED FISH WITH HORSERADISH CREAM SAUCE

1 - 1¼ lb. any white-meat fish filets
¼ c. chicken stock or white wine
1½ tsp. fresh lemon juice
1 T. + 2 tsp. margarine

1 T. flour
¼ c. whipping cream
1½ tsp. grated horseradish root
salt

Preheat oven to 400°. Place the fish in a greased 1½-qt. casserole dish. Add chicken stock or wine, lemon juice. Bake uncovered for 15 minutes. Remove fish and set on plate. Melt margarine in a small saucepan over medium heat. Add flour and stir to incorporate. Gradually add ½ c. liquid from the baked fish and discard remaining liquid. Stir to prevent clumping. Add cream, horseradish and salt, again stirring until thickened. Place fish back into the casserole dish and cover fish with the cooked sauce. Bake uncovered in a 400° oven for 10 minutes to heat through. Serves 2.

60736D-02

ORIENTAL HALIBUT

½ c. pineapple juice
1 T. soy sauce
½ of garlic clove, pressed
¼ tsp. grated ginger root
salt
¼ tsp. sesame oil
1 tsp. cornstarch

1 T. water
half can of coconut milk
1 T. finely chopped pecans or
walnuts
1-1¼ lbs. barbecued or baked
halibut

In a small saucepan combine pineapple juice, soy sauce, garlic, ginger, salt and sesame oil. Bring to a boil and simmer 5 minutes, stirring occasionally. In small bowl blend cornstarch, water and coconut milk until smooth. Whisk into hot juice mixture. Stir until thickened and starts to boil. Pour over halibut and top with chopped walnuts or pecans. Serves 2-3.

CHICKEN SMOTHERED IN MUSTARD-DILL SAUCE OVER RICE

1-1½ c. cooked rice
1 tsp. olive oil
2 boneless, skinless chicken
breast halves
1 T. + 1½ tsp. margarine
1 T. + 1½ tsp. flour
¼ c. + 1 T. milk

¼ c. sour cream
one quarter of chicken bouillon
cube
1 T. + 1 tsp. Dijon mustard
¼ tsp. dill weed
half of small garlic clove, pressed
salt

Cook rice according to directions. In the meantime, in medium sauté pan brown the chicken breast on both sides in olive oil until thoroughly cooked. Remove chicken and set aside. Cover with foil or a lid to keep warm. Add margarine to sauté pan and melt over medium heat. Add flour and stir until smooth. Gradually stir in milk. Then stir in sour cream and partial bouillon cube. Mash bouillon cube with the back of a spoon. Add mustard, dill, garlic and salt. Stir and cook until thickened but do not let boil. Spoon rice onto plate. Set chicken breast on rice and top with sauce. Serves 2.

60736D-02

BROILED OR BARBECUED PRAWNS WITH LIME BUTTER

¼ c. butter
¼ c. dry white wine
2 T. fresh lime juice
1½ tsp. honey

half of small garlic clove, pressed
6-8 large prawns, peeled and
  deveined
1 green onion, sliced

Put butter, wine, lime juice, honey, and garlic in small saucepan, Heat over low heat for about 3 minutes. Place prawns on broiler pan or on the barbecue. Brush with some of the lime butter. Broil or barbecue, turning prawns every 2 minutes until prawn meat just turns opaque. Baste each time you turn the prawns. Sprinkle with green onion before serving. Serves 2.

SHRIMP IN ORANGE-THYME SAUCE

1 tsp. orange zest
½ navel orange
1 c. whipping cream
¼ tsp. thyme
1 garlic clove, pressed

¾ lb. fresh medium shrimp with
  shells
¼ tsp. salt
1½ c. cooked rice

Peel and devein shrimp, reserving shells. Grate orange zest and set aside. Slice ½ orange into thin crosswise slices. Trim white pith and peel from the outside of slices and quarter each slice. In a medium saucepan combine cream, orange zest, thyme, garlic and shrimp shells. Bring to a boil over medium heat. Then reduce heat to simmer cream mixture until it is reduced to about ¾ c. This should take about 13 minutes. Remove the shells with slotted spoon and discard. Add the shrimp to the saucepan and heat over medium heat just until the shrimp meat turns opaque. Season with salt. Serve over cooked rice. Arrange orange slices next to the shrimp. Serves 2.

60736D-02

SOFT TACOS

1 lb. ground sirloin
1 clove garlic, pressed
3 T. chopped onion
½ tsp. hot sauce
1 tsp. chili powder
¼ tsp. salt

4-5 8-inch flour tortillas
1 tomato, chopped
1 c. chopped lettuce
¾ c. shredded cheddar cheese
½ c. salsa or picante sauce

In medium fry pan brown the ground sirloin with the garlic and onion. When meat is thoroughly cooked drain and discard any grease. Add hot sauce, chili powder and salt. Stir and heat to serving temperature. On a heated nonstick griddle or 10-inch fry pan place a tortilla that has been slightly moistened with water (I usually wet one of my hands under the faucet and wipe each side of the tortilla) before placing it on the heated griddle or fry pan. Warm each side of the tortilla a few seconds. Put on a plate and spread a layer of the following down the middle: meat mixture, chopped tomato, chopped lettuce, shredded cheese and salsa. Fold over the two outside edges. Makes 4-5 tacos.

CREAMY BEEF AND TOMATO CASSEROLE

4 oz. dry noodles (any size or
   shape)
½ lb. ground sirloin
half of 8-oz. can tomato sauce
½ c. water
½ tsp. salt

⅛ tsp. pepper
4 oz. cream cheese
½ c. cottage cheese
2 T. sour cream
¼ c. chopped onion
4 mushrooms, chopped

Preheat oven to 350°. Grease 1½-qt. casserole dish. Cook noodles in water as directed on package in a large saucepan. While noodles are cooking brown ground sirloin breaking chunks with the back of a spoon. Add tomato sauce, water, salt, pepper, cream cheese, cottage cheese, sour cream, onion and mushrooms. Stir to incorporate. When noodles are done drain and discard water. Add meat sauce and stir to incorporate all ingredients. Pour into casserole dish and bake for 45 min. Serves 3.

60736D-02

ARTICHOKE AND LEMON PASTA

14³/₄-oz. can chicken stock
9 oz. any style dry pasta
2 T. dehydrated sun dried
   tomatoes
¼ c. sliced green onions
½ tsp. crushed rosemary

1 small clove garlic, pressed
13³/₄-oz. can artichoke hearts,
   drained and chopped
½ c. dry white wine
1 tsp. grated lemon peel
¼ c. whipping cream

In a medium saucepan bring the chicken stock to a boil. Add pasta, sun-dried tomatoes and stir. Simmer 4-5 minutes until pasta is tender but firm. Add green onions, rosemary, garlic, artichoke hearts, wine and lemon peel. Stir until just boiling. Add cream and warm to serving temperature but do not boil. Serves 2-3.

SALMON ON A BED OF GREENS WITH LIME-GINGER DRESSING

Dressing:

²/₃ c. fresh lime juice
½ c. honey

½ tsp. fresh grated ginger
⅛ tsp. salt

In a jar with lid shake all the ingredients until well mixed.

Salmon:

1-1½ lb. salmon filet

Marinate salmon in half the dressing for 4-5 hours reserving the remaining dressing for the salad. Barbecue or bake just until salmon meat is opaque and flakey.

Salad Bed:

2½ c. assorted lettuces, broken
   into bite-size pieces

¼ c. peeled and sliced cucumber
⅓ c. diced pear, apple or mango

On dinner plate place the lettuces, cucumber and diced fruit. On top of that place the warm salmon. Then drizzle some of the reserved dressing. Serve immediately. Serves 2.

60736D-02

FAJITAS

Meat:

½ lb. flank or round steak	⅛ tsp. chili powder
¼ c. fresh lime juice	1 small clove garlic, pressed
1 T. tequila (optional)	⅓ c. sliced sweet onion
⅛ tsp. cumin	

Trim excess fat from the steak and pound meat with meat mallet or edge of saucer to ¼- inch thick. Cut into ½-inch strips. Combine meat, lime juice, tequila, cumin, chili powder, garlic and onion in quart-size resealable bag or 1½-qt. casserole dish. Seal bag or cover casserole dish. Marinate 6 - 8 hours at least.

Guacamole:

1 avocado	1 small clove garlic, pressed
3 T. salsa or picante sauce	⅛ tsp. chili powder
1 tsp. fresh lime juice	

Slice avocado lengthwise and remove seed with a spoon. Scoop the avocado meat out out of the shell with a spoon into a small bowl. Add salsa (or picante sauce), lime juice, garlic and chili powder. Mash avocado with a fork and stir to combine all ingredients.

Garnishes:

3 8-inch flour tortillas	4 T. salsa or picante sauce
1 tomato, diced	3 T. sour cream

In large fry pan heat marinated meat and veggies over medium heat, stirring frequently. When meat is thoroughly cooked set pan aside. Warm tortillas by wiping your wet hand over each side of the tortilla before placing it on a warmed nonstick griddle or fry pan. Warm about 20 seconds on each side. Scoop cooked meat and veggie mixture down the center of a warm tortilla, top with guacamole and tomato, salsa (or picante sauce) and sour cream. Fold the two outer edges in toward center to cover filling. Serves 2-3.

60736D-02

PORK OR CHICKEN QUESADILLAS

1 tsp. fresh lime juice
¼ c. sour cream
1 lb. leftover barbecued or baked
    pork or chicken, shredded or
    cut into bite-size chunks
4 8-inch flour tortillas
¾ c. shredded mozzarella,
    cheddar or jack cheese or
    crumbled ricotta cheese

¼ c. chopped onion
¼ c. chopped tomato
2 T. chopped cilantro
3 T. chopped black olives

Mix together the lime juice and sour cream in a small cup or dish. Set aside. On heated nonstick griddle place one tortilla. Spread one half each of the meat, cheese, onion, tomato, cilantro and olives evenly on top. Place another tortilla on top and loosely tent a piece of foil over the griddle to hold heat. Heat until cheese is melted. Turn with a pancake turner and warm the second side. Place heated quesadilla on a cutting board and cut into wedges. Repeat with the remaining ingredients. Place a dollop of sour cream mixture on top of each wedge. Serves 2.

60736D-02

GERMAN SOUR CREAM AND DILL PORK CHOPS

Pork Cutlets:

2 boneless pork loin chops, trimmed	1 egg, beaten
2 T. flour	1 T. milk
½ tsp. salt	⅓ c. dry bread crumbs
⅛ tsp. pepper	½ tsp. paprika
	1½ tsp. cooking oil

Pound pork chops with a mallet or edge of a saucer until they are ¼ inch thick. In a small bowl mix together the flour, salt and pepper. In another small bowl mix the egg and milk. In a third small bowl mix together the dry bread crumbs and paprika. Dredge the chops first in the flour mixture, then in the egg mixture and finally in the bread crumb mixture. Place in heated fry pan with the cooking oil. Brown 3 minutes on each side or until chops are cooked through. Remove and keep warm while making the sauce.

Sour Cream and Dill Sauce:

½ c. chicken stock	¼ tsp. dry dill weed
2 tsp. flour	⅓ c. sour cream

Pour chicken stock into the fry pan with the drippings. Scrape the sides and bottom of the pan to loosen the crusty drippings. In a cup mix together the flour, sour cream and dill weed. Pour a little of the chicken stock into the cup and stir to incorporate. Then add to the stock, stirring while the sauce warms. Do not boil. Serve the sauce on top of the chops. Serves 2.

60736D-02

PORK CHOPS IN ORANGE SAUCE

2 tsp. cooking oil	3 T. water
2 pork chops	½ tsp. grated orange zest
2 orange slices (crosswise)	2 T. orange juice
1 thin slice onion	2 tsp. lemon juice
2 T. brown sugar	1½ tsp. cornstarch

Brown pork chops in cooking oil in medium fry pan. Top each chop with an orange slice and half the onion slice. Mix together brown sugar, water and orange zest. Pour over the pork chops. Cover and cook for 20 minutes until done. Remove chops, orange and onion slices. Keep warm while making the sauce. Mix together the orange juice, lemon juice and cornstarch. Pour into the juices in the fry pan. Stir constantly until sauce comes to a boil. Serve sauce over the chops. Serves 2.

PORK CHOPS SMOTHERED IN CARAMELIZED ONIONS

½ c. flour	½ tsp. sugar
2 1-inch thick boneless loin pork chops	1 clove garlic, pressed
1½ T. cooking oil	14¼-oz. can beef stock
½ tsp. Hungarian paprika	⅓ c. grated smoked Gouda cheese
1 c. sliced onions	

Dredge pork chops in flour and brown with cooking oil in medium fry pan over medium heat. Cook 3 minutes per side. Sprinkle with paprika. Remove chops and keep warm. In the fry pan put the onion, sugar and garlic. Sauté until well browned (about 15 minutes). Add 1 T. of the leftover flour to the pan and stir to incorporate. Add stock and stir well. Place chops in fry pan with stock mixture. Cover and cook for 12 minutes. Remove lid and reduce sauce to 1 cup. Top with cheese and serve. Serves 2.

60736D-02

GRAMPY'S MEAT LOAF

1½ lb. ground sirloin
¾ c. oatmeal
2 eggs, beaten
¼ c. onion, chopped

1 tsp. salt
¼ tsp. pepper
8-oz. can tomato sauce

Preheat oven to 350°. Grease 9x5x3-inch loaf pan. In medium bowl mix together ground sirloin, oatmeal, eggs, onion, salt, pepper and tomato sauce. With your hands form an oblong-shaped loaf and place loaf pan. Bake in 350° oven for 1 hour. Serves 6 or, if fewer, there will be plenty of leftover meat loaf for sandwiches.

PECAN ENCRUSTED PORK TENDERLOIN WITH GARLIC-GINGER MAYONNAISE

Ginger and Garlic Mayonnaise:

1 tsp. peeled and grated fresh
  ginger
1 large garlic clove, pressed
¼ c. pasteurized egg
4 tsp. white wine vinegar

⅛ tsp. salt
¾ c. + 2½ T. peanut oil
1½ T. sesame oil
4 drops hot sauce

Preheat oven to 375°. Blender ginger, garlic, egg, vinegar and salt in blender until smooth. With the machine running slowly add both oils. Process until thick. Add hot sauce and blend to mix. Transfer to a small bowl, cover and refrigerate before serving.

Pecan Encrusted Pork Tenderloin:

½ c. pecans, finely chopped
⅓ c. fine dry breadcrumbs
½ c. flour
salt and pepper

4 T. pasteurized egg
1½ lb. pork tenderloin
3 T. olive oil
1 green onion, sliced

Combine pecans and breadcrumbs in a medium bowl. Place flour in shallow dish. Put beaten egg in a second shallow dish. Dredge pork in flour, then in beaten egg and last in the pecan-bread crumb mixture. Heat oil in heavy ovenproof skillet. Add pork and brown 3 minutes per side. Place skillet in oven for about 8 minutes until pork is done. Cut into ¼-inch thick slices and serve slices fanned out on plates for serving. Top with Garlic-Ginger Mayonnaise and sliced green onion. Serves 3-4.

60736D-02

PORK CUTLETS WITH CREAMY SAGE SAUCE

2 boneless loin pork chops	½ c. chicken stock
1 tsp. sage	1 T. maple syrup
salt and pepper	1 T. Dijon or course-grained
1 T. margarine	mustard

On a cutting board pound the pork chops with a mallet or edge of a saucer until the chops are ¼-inch thick. Sprinkle with ½ tsp. sage, salt and pepper. Melt margarine in a heavy skillet over medium heat. Add pork and cook until brown on both sides and thoroughly cooked (about 1½ minutes per side). Transfer to a plate. Add chicken stock, maple syrup, mustard and remaining ½ tsp. sage. Stir and bring to a boil. Reduce heat to low. Return pork to skillet with any accumulated juices. Cook until just heated through. Serve pork with sauce. Serves 2.

PORK TENDERLOIN WITH APPLE AND BRANDY SAUCE

1 lb. pork tenderloin, cut into	¾ tsp. sugar
1-inch thick slices	¼ c. onion, chopped
4 T. margarine	¾ tsp. thyme
3 medium Golden Delicious	3 T. brandy
apples, peeled, cored and sliced	¾ c. whipping cream
¼-inch thick	3 T. apple juice

On a cutting board pound pork slices with a meat mallet or edge of a saucer until it is ¼-inch thick. Melt 2 T. margarine in heavy skillet over medium heat. Add apple slices and sugar and sauté until golden brown (about 5-6 minutes). Remove apple mixture and place in a bowl. Put 1 T. margarine in the skillet with the pork medallions. Brown 2 minutes per side. Remove pork and set on plate. In skillet add the remaining 1 T. margarine, onion and thyme. Sauté 2 minutes. Add brandy and reduce to a glaze while stirring browned drippings from the bottom of the pan. Stir in cream and apple juice. Boil until the mixture thickens (about 3 minutes). Add apple mixture and pork. Reheat to serving temperature. Serves 2-3.

60736D-02

PORK MEDALLIONS WITH MUSHROOMS

¾ lb. pork tenderloin
2 T. flour
¼ tsp. salt
pepper
6 tsp. olive oil
3 tsp. butter
2 medium cloves garlic, pressed

½ c. minced onion
8 mushrooms, sliced
¼ tsp. rosemary
½ c. chicken stock
⅓ c. dry white wine
1½ T. capers

Cut pork into ½-inch diagonal slices. Pound to ⅛ inch thick with a mallet or edge of a saucer. Dredge half of pork slices in flour and place in preheated heavy skillet with 2 teaspoons olive oil. Cook on medium heat for 2 minutes per side. Remove from pan and keep warm. Repeat with remaining pork adding another 2 teaspoons of olive oil. Add remaining 2 teaspoons olive oil and 2 teaspoons of butter to the pan with garlic and onion. Sauté 1 minute. Add mushrooms and sprinkle with salt, pepper and rosemary. Sauté 5 minutes. Remove from pan. Pour chicken stock and wine into pan with the remaining 1 teaspoon butter. Cook for 2 minutes. Pour mushrooms and sauce over pork. Top with capers and serve. Serves 4.

MARGARITA CHICKEN BREAST

½ tsp. jalapeño pepper, minced
   with seeds and pith removed
2 tsp. tequila
1½ tsp. olive oil
1½ tsp. fresh lime juice
1 tsp. chopped fresh parsley

½ tsp. dried tarragon
½ tsp. honey
¼ tsp. salt
pepper
2 boneless, skinless chicken
   breast halves

Mix all the ingredients except the chicken breasts in a resealable plastic bag. Then add the chicken breasts and marinate overnight. Barbecue until done. In the meantime, heat the leftover marinade to a boil and serve over the chicken. Serves 2.

60736D-02

DIETER'S DELIGHT CHICKEN BREAST

1 c. finely chopped mushrooms
½ medium onion, minced
1 garlic clove, pressed
2 boneless, skinless chicken
   breast halves
1 T. Dijon mustard

1 T. capers
½ tsp. balsamic vinegar
3 dashes hot sauce
1 T. mayonnaise
salt

Preheat oven to 375°. Place chicken breasts in a greased 8x8-inch baking dish. Heat in oven for 10 minutes. In a medium nonstick sauté pan stir mushrooms, onion, and garlic over medium heat until slightly brown. Stir the mustard, capers, vinegar, hot sauce and mayonnaise in with the mushrooms. Spread the mushroom mixture over the top of the chicken breasts and return to the oven for 15-20 minutes until the meat is no longer pink inside. Add salt to taste. Serves 2.

PARMESAN BAKED CHICKEN

⅓ c. dry bread crumbs
⅓ c. shredded Parmesan cheese
salt & pepper
⅛ tsp. garlic powder
¾ c. dry white wine

2 drops hot sauce
2 boneless, skinless chicken
   breast halves
1½ T. margarine, melted

Preheat oven to 350°. Grease an 8x8-inch baking dish. In a medium shallow bowl combine the bread crumbs, Parmesan cheese, salt, pepper and garlic powder. In another medium bowl stir together the wine and hot sauce. Rinse and pat dry the chicken with a paper towel. Dip the chicken first into the wine mixture and then into the bread crumb mixture. Place chicken on the baking dish. Drizzle the melted margarine over the chicken and bake for 45 minutes or until the meat is no longer pink inside. Serves 2.

60736D-02

SPICY PEANUT CHICKEN

2 boneless, skinless chicken breast halves, cut into ½-inch strips	1½ T. peanut oil (or cooking oil)
2 tsp. fresh lime juice	¼ tsp. fresh grated ginger root
2 garlic cloves, pressed	14½. oz.-can chicken stock
3 T. soy sauce	3 or 4 T. peanut butter (preferably old fashion style)
¼ tsp. red pepper flakes	1 green onion, sliced

Place the chicken breasts, lime juice, only 1 of the garlic cloves, soy sauce, only 2 T. soy sauce and red pepper flakes in a resealable plastic bag. Marinate the chicken breasts for a at least 4 hours. In medium fry pan sauté the remaining garlic clove in the peanut oil. When slightly browned add the chicken strips and cook until almost done. Add half of the marinade (be sure to get half of the "goodies" from the marinade and not just the liquid), the remaining 1 T. soy sauce, ginger, chicken stock and peanut butter. Stir to mix together. Heat over medium-low heat and stir while warming. Sauce will thicken as it warms. Stirring will prevent the sauce from sticking to the bottom. Top with green onion when serving. Serves 2.

CHICKEN TO DIE FOR

1 large garlic clove, pressed	1 c. + whipping cream
1 slice bacon, chopped	¼ tsp. rosemary
6 oz. mushrooms, sliced	¼ c. pitted Greek or Kalamata olives, chopped
3 T. flour	
½ chicken, cut into parts	

In medium fry pan sauté garlic and bacon until bacon is cooked. Add mushrooms and cook just until slightly softened. Remove and set aside. Flour chicken parts in the flour by tossing together in a bag. In the drippings fry the chicken parts and cook thoroughly. Remove. Put cream in the pan and return the bacon mixture along with rosemary and olives. Reduce sauce until it becomes thickened. Add chicken and warm to serving temperature. Serves 2.

60736D-02

ROASTED CHICKEN WITH GARLIC MAYONNAISE

Garlic Mayonnaise:

½ c. mayonnaise	½ tsp. Dijon mustard
½ tsp. thyme	1½ tsp. fresh lemon juice
½ a garlic clove, pressed	

Stir together all the ingredients and refrigerate until ready to serve.

Roasted Chicken:

1 T. olive oil	salt and pepper
2 boneless, skinless chicken breast halves	⅔ c. artichoke hearts, chopped
	¼ c. sun dried tomatoes

Preheat oven to 400°. Grease 9x5x3-inch loaf pan. Reconstitute the tomatoes by soaking them in boiling water while you move onto the next step in preparation. In medium fry pan heat the olive oil over medium heat. Season the chicken with salt and pepper. Put into fry pan and brown both sides. When done place in loaf pan. Then top with artichokes and tomatoes. Put pan in oven and roast for 15 minutes or until cooked through. Serve with Garlic Mayonnaise on the side. Serves 2.

INDIAN SPICED CHICKEN BREASTS

2 boneless, skinless chicken breast halves	¼ tsp. cumin
	⅛ tsp. cinnamon
½ c. plain yogurt	⅛ tsp. cayenne pepper
1 T. fresh grated ginger	⅛ tsp. turmeric
1½ tsp. fresh lime juice	salt and pepper

Grease a 9x5x3-inch loaf pan. Place chicken in pan. Stir together the yogurt, ginger, lime juice, cumin, cinnamon, cayenne pepper, turmeric, salt and pepper. Spoon over the top of the chicken breasts and cover completely. Cover and refrigerate 3 to 24 hours. Bake in preheated 375° oven for 30 minutes until done. Serve with INDIAN SPICED RICE. Serves 2.

60736D-02

AL'S FAVORITE CHICKEN-AVOCADO SANDWICH

Sauce:

⅓ c. salsa   1 green onion, sliced
⅓ c. mayonnaise

Stir all ingredients together, cover and keep in refrigerator until ready to serve.

Chicken-Avocado Sandwich:

2 toasted English muffins   ½ c. chopped mushrooms
1½ c. cooked (baked, roasted or   ½ avocado, thinly sliced
   barbecued) chicken breast meat 6 slices of cheddar or jack cheese

Place English muffin halves on cookie sheet. Top with chicken meat, mushrooms, avocados and cheese slices. Place under broiler until cheese is bubbly and turning golden brown. Top with sauce. Serves 2-3.

CHICKEN WITH TARRAGON CREAM SAUCE

1½ tsp. olive oil   ⅓ c. whipping cream
2 boneless, skinless chicken   2 tsp. capers
   breast halves   ½ tsp. fresh lemon juice
salt and pepper   ¼ tsp. tarragon
1½ tsp. olive oil   1 T. margarine

In medium fry pan heat olive oil over medium heat. Add chicken and cook about 5 minutes per side or cooked through. Season with salt and pepper. Remove from the pan and keep warm. In the pan add cream, capers, lemon juice and tarragon. Stir any browned drippings into the cream sauce. Keep stirring until the sauce just comes to a boil. Remove from the heat and stir in the margarine and any juices that have accumulated on the chicken plate. Pour sauce over the chicken. Serves 2.

60736D-02

SINGAPORE CHICKEN

¼ c. fresh orange juice
2 T. fresh lime juice
1½ T. mango chutney
1½ tsp. grated fresh ginger
2½ tsp. rice vinegar
2 tsp. orange zest

1¾ tsp. sesame oil
pinch of red pepper flakes
½ chicken, cut into pieces
salt and pepper
3 to 4 T. sesame seeds

Preheat oven to 350°. Grease an 8x8-inch baking dish. Mix together the orange juice, lime juice, chutney, ginger, vinegar, orange zest, ¾ tsp. sesame oil and red pepper flakes in the baking dish. Set aside. In a medium nonstick fry pan heat remaining 1 tsp. sesame oil over medium heat. Salt and pepper the chicken pieces and dredge in sesame seeds before browning in the hot oil. Once all sides of the chicken is browned place chicken in the baking dish and cover with foil. Bake in oven for 25 minutes. Remove foil and bake for an additional 20 minutes or until chicken is done. Serve hot or cold. Serves 2.

CHICKEN AND PINEAPPLE KABOBS

2 boneless, skinless chicken
  breast halves, cut into 1½-inch
  chunks
⅓ bell pepper, seeds removed
  and cut into 1½-inch chunks
½ of 20-oz. can pineapple chunks
1 T. brown sugar

1 T. soy sauce
2 T. pineapple juice
2 tsp. fresh lime juice
2 tsp. grated fresh ginger
2 tsp. sesame oil
1 tsp. curry
1 clove garlic, pressed

Place all ingredients in a resealable plastic bag. Mix together well and refrigerate to marinate for at least 6 hours. Thread chicken, green pepper and pineapple on skewers. Barbecue until chicken is done turning every 3 minutes. Serves 2.

60736D-02

CHICKEN IN CHUTNEY CREAM SAUCE

1 tsp. cooking oil
2 boneless, skinless chicken
   breast halves
salt & pepper
1 shallot (or ¼ c. onion), minced
1 small garlic clove, pressed
1 tsp. fresh grated ginger

½ c. chicken stock
½ c. whipping cream
½ tsp. cornstarch
½ tsp. mango chutney
2 tsp. fresh lemon juice
½ tsp. basil

In a medium nonstick fry pan heat the oil over medium heat. Add chicken breasts and sauté for 4-5 minutes per side or until cooked through. Season with salt and pepper. Remove from pan. Put shallot (or onion), garlic, ginger and a couple of tablespoons of the chicken stock in the pan. Cook for 1 minute in pan. Add the remaining stock and cook another 2 minutes. Combine the whipping cream and cornstarch. Add to the pan and cook to a boil. Reduce 1-2 minutes until the sauce has started to thicken. Stir in the chutney, lemon juice and basil. Add any juices that may have collected from the chicken on the plate. Cook 30 seconds. Serve over rice. Serves 2.

CHICKEN WITH BACON AND POTATOES

2 red skinned-potatoes, dice into
   ¾-inch pieces
2 slices bacon, cut into ½-inch
   pieces
2 boneless, skinless chicken
   breast halves

salt and pepper
1 c. fresh or frozen pearl onions
   (thawed)
⅓ c. chicken stock
½ tsp. thyme
chopped parsley

In medium saucepan boil potatoes in water for 4 minutes. In the meantime, sauté bacon in a medium fry pan. When brown remove bacon and drain on paper towel. Season chicken with salt and pepper. Cook over medium heat in the fry pan with bacon drippings for about 2 minutes per side. Reduce heat to low. Add potatoes, onions, stock and thyme. Cover and simmer until chicken is cooked through and potatoes are tender (about 18 minutes). Uncover and sprinkle with bacon bits and cook until sauce thickens slightly. Baste chicken occasionally. Serve and top with parsley. Serves 2.

60736D-02

ASPARAGUS AND PENNE

4 oz. penne pasta
1 c. asparagus, cut in 1-inch
  pieces
1½ T. olive oil
1 clove garlic, pressed

1 T. balsamic vinegar
small-medium tomato, diced
salt and pepper
2 T. fresh grated Parmesan or
  Romano cheese

In a medium saucepan cook the pasta. During the last 3 minutes of cooking time add the asparagus. When both are tender drain. Add olive oil and garlic. Cook over medium heat for 1 minute, stirring constantly. Add vinegar, tomatoes salt and pepper. Cook about 2 minutes until tomatoes are warm. Add cheese and toss. Serves 2.

HAVARTI STUFFED CHICKEN BREASTS

2 chicken breast halves
2 slices Havarti cheese
⅛ tsp. dill

½ garlic clove, pressed
1 T. olive oil
salt and pepper

Lay the chicken breast on a flat surface. Make a slit through the breast horizontally to make a pocket. Sprinkle the dill inside of the pocket. Then place slice of cheese in it. In small nonstick fry pan heat oil and lightly brown the garlic. Place stuffed chicken breasts in fry pan and brown 6 minutes on each side until cooked through. Sprinkle with salt and pepper. Serves 2.

SCALLOPS IN WINE AND BUTTER SAUCE

1 c. dry white wine
½ tsp. grated lemon peel
¾ lb. fresh scallops
1½ tsp. Dijon mustard

4 T. real butter
salt and pepper
2 c. cooked pasta or rice

Bring wine and lemon peel to simmer in a medium fry pan over medium heat. Add scallops and cook until almost opaque. Remove with a slotted spoon. Reduce the wine mixture to ¼ cup. Then reduce heat to low. Stir in mustard and 1 tablespoon of butter at a time until melted. Add scallops and any juices and heat through. Season with salt and pepper. Serve over cooked pasta or rice. Serves 2.

60736D-02

ITALIAN CHICKEN

10-oz. package frozen chopped
   spinach, thawed
3-oz. package cream cheese,
   room temperature
¼ c. dry bread crumbs
1 tsp. Italian seasoning
⅛ tsp. oregano

2 tsp. olive oil
2 chicken breasts
½ c. shredded mozzarella cheese
2 tomato slices
2 T. fresh grated Parmesan
   cheese

Preheat oven to 350°. Grease 9x5x3-inch loaf pan. Squeeze spinach in your hands to remove water. Mix together spinach and cream cheese in a medium bowl. Press into bottom of loaf pan. In a medium bowl combine the bread crumbs with Italian seasoning and oregano. Roll chicken in the bread crumb mixture. Brown the chicken in hot olive oil in a small nonstick fry pan. Cook 2 minutes per side over medium heat until browned. Place chicken on top of the spinach mixture and top with the mozzarella cheese. Place a tomato slice on top of each chicken breast. Combine the Parmesan cheese with the remaining bread crumbs and sprinkle over the top. Bake in oven for 30 minutes. Serves 2.

FETA AND ARTICHOKE STUFFED CHICKEN POCKETS

2 chicken breast halves, sliced
   horizontally to make a pocket
¼ c. crumbled feta cheese
¼ of 13¾-oz. can artichoke
   hearts, chopped fine

1 small clove garlic, pressed
2 T. fresh shredded Parmesan or
   Romano cheese

Preheat oven to 350°. Grease a 9x5x3-inch loaf pan. Slice chicken breast horizontally on the one thick side to form a pocket in the middle. In a small bowl mix together the feta cheese, artichoke hearts and garlic. Stuff the chicken breasts with the cheese mixture. Place stuffed breast pockets into pan and sprinkle the Parmesan (or Romano) on top of each. Bake for about 35 minutes or until cooked through. Serves 2.

60736D-02

DEVONSHIRE SANDWICH

Sandwich:

2 slices toast	1-2 cooked chicken breasts,
4 slices bacon, fried and drained	sliced

Place toast on a cookie sheet. Top with bacon and sliced chicken.

Cheese Sauce:

2½ T. margarine	heavy pinch of poultry seasoning
2½ T. flour	1 c. shredded cheddar cheese
1 c. milk	1 T. fresh grated Parmesan or
⅛ tsp. salt	Romano cheese
heavy pinch of dry mustard	

Preheat oven to 350°. In a small saucepan melt the margarine. Stir in the flour. Add the milk, salt, mustard and poultry seasoning and stir. Heat over medium heat, stirring as the sauce thickens. Add cheddar cheese and stir until cheese is melted. Pour sauce over the sandwiches and top with Parmesan cheese. Place sandwiches in the oven for about 10 minutes until bubbly. Serves 2.

STUFFED ZUCCHINI

2 medium zucchini	1 small clove garlic, pressed
¼ c. chopped onion	½ lb. seasoned ground sausage,
¼ c. dry bread crumbs	cooked and drained
½ tsp. Italian seasoning	¼ tsp. thyme
2 T. fresh grated Parmesan	¼ tsp. oregano
cheese	salt and pepper
1 egg, beaten	⅓ c. shredded cheddar cheese

Bring large saucepan of water to boil. Add zucchini and cook until just tender (about 15 minutes). Remove from water with slotted spoon. Preheat oven to 350°. Line 8x8-inch baking dish with foil. Cool zucchini slightly, cut lengthwise and scoop out pulp. Mix the zucchini pulp in a medium bowl with the onion, bread crumbs, Italian seasoning, Parmesan cheese, egg, garlic, cooked sausage, thyme, oregano, salt, pepper and cheddar cheese. Spoon mixture into the zucchini shells. Place in baking dish and bake for 20 minutes until golden brown on top. Serves 2-3.

60736D-02

CHICKEN PICCATA

2 boneless, skinless chicken
   breast halves
3 T. real butter

1 T. fresh lemon juice
2 tsp. capers

In fry pan melt butter over medium heat. Add chicken and brown on both sides. Make sure chicken is cooked through. Put chicken on serving plates. Add lemon juice to pan and heat to warm. Pour over the chicken. Top with capers. Serves 2.

PORK CHOPS WITH MUSTARD-SAGE BUTTER

2 tsp. crumbled sage
1 clove garlic, pressed
fresh ground pepper
2 thick cut boneless pork chops
2 tsp. balsamic vinegar

1 T. olive oil
3 T. butter
2 tsp. Dijon mustard
2 tsp. minced fresh parsley
½ tsp. crumbled sage

Combine 2 tsp. sage, garlic and pepper. Set Aside. Rub pork chops with vinegar, then oil. Let stand at least 30 minutes or up to 2 hours. Meanwhile combine butter, mustard, parsley and ½ tsp. sage. Season butter mixture with pepper. Preheat broiler or barbecue. Cook chops about 7 minutes per side or until done. Top each with a dollop of mustard-sage butter before serving. Serves 2.

60736D-02

SHEPHERDS PIE WITH GARLIC-MASHED POTATOES

Filling:

½ lb. ground lamb (or ground beef)
¼ lb. ground Italian sausage
½ medium onion, chopped
½ medium carrot, sliced crosswise into ¼-inch slices

1 small garlic clove, pressed
½ tsp. crushed rosemary
¼ tsp. turmeric
¼ tsp. cinnamon
2 tsp. flour
½ c. beef stock

Preheat oven to 350°. Grease 1½-qt casserole dish. In large fry pan cook ground lamb (or ground beef) and Italian sausage, breaking the meat chunks with the back of spoon. Drain off all fat but 1½ T. of drippings. Add onion, carrot, garlic, rosemary, turmeric and cinnamon. Simmer for 5 minutes. Add flour and stir into the spicy meat mixture. Add beef stock and stir to incorporate. Cover fry pan and cook until carrot is just tender (about 13 minutes). Pour filling into the casserole dish.

Mashed Potato Top:

1 large or 2 small russet potatoes, cut into 1-inch chunks
1 clove garlic, peeled

2 T. margarine
3 T. half and half

Boil potatoes and garlic in medium covered saucepan until done. Drain. Then add margarine and half and half before mashing potatoes. Spoon mashed potatoes on top of filling in casserole dish. Bake in oven for 25-30 minutes until mashed potato top is slightly brown. Serves 2.

60736D-02

SPINACH-RICOTTA STUFFED PASTA SHELLS

Spinach Filling:

10-oz. pkg. frozen chopped
   spinach, thawed and pressed dry
6 tsp. margarine
3 T. chopped onion
1 clove garlic, pressed
½ c. cooked chopped ham or
   sausage

⅛ tsp. nutmeg
¼ c. ricotta cheese
½ c. freshly grated Parmesan
   cheese
2 T. chopped sun dried tomatoes
   (optional)
1 egg

Preheat oven to 375°. Grease a 9x5x3-inch loaf pan. In a medium fry pan mix together spinach with 2 tsp. margarine, turning frequently until moisture has evaporated. Remove from fry pan and set aside. Put remaining margarine in fry pan and sauté garlic and onion until clear. Add ham (or sausage) and sauté 1 minute. Return spinach to fry pan. Add nutmeg and mix. Remove from heat and cool slightly. Stir in ricotta and Parmesan cheeses, optional sun dried tomatoes and egg.

Bechamel Sauce:

2 T. margarine
2 T. flour

1 chicken bouillon cube
¾ c. milk

Melt margarine in small saucepan. Add flour and stir to incorporate. Add bouillon cube, mash with back of spoon and stir to mix. Add milk and stir over medium heat until sauce starts to boil. Remove from heat.

Shell Pasta:

6 shell-shaped pasta

Boil pasta shells in water until slightly tender. Drain. To assemble: Put half of bechamel sauce in bottom of loaf pan. Fill shells with the spinach filling and place on sauce in pan. Pour remaining sauce on top of the stuffed shells.

Topping:

⅓ c. freshly grated Parmesan
cheese

Top with the ⅓ c. Parmesan cheese. Bake for 20-25 minutes. Serves 3.

60736D-02

MUSTARD VINAIGRETTE ROASTED CHICKEN AND POTATO SALAD

Mustard Vinaigrette:

3 T. Dijon mustard	1/2 c. chopped shallots (or onions)
2 1/2 T. wine vinegar	1/2 tsp. crushed rosemary
2/3 c. olive oil	1/2 tsp. sage

In a small bowl combine all the ingredients.

Potato Salad:

1 lb. red or white baby potatoes	1/4 c. peas
2 or 3 T. Mustard Vinaigrette	1/4 c. chopped walnuts (or pecans)
1/3 c. crumbled blue cheese	

In a medium bowl toss potatoes in Mustard Vinaigrette. Set aside.

Roasted Chicken:

1/2 chicken	2 T. Mustard Vinaigrette
salt and pepper	

Preheat oven to 450°. Grease 8x8-inch baking dish. Put 2 T. Mustard Vinaigrette under the chicken skin and rub more on the surface of the chicken. Sprinkle with salt and pepper. Place in baking dish. Once again toss the potatoes with the Mustard Vinaigrette in the bowl. Spoon potatoes into the baking dish with the chicken. Reserve Mustard Vinaigrette for basting chicken every 15 minutes during roasting. Bake in oven for 50-60 minutes. Remove potatoes when cooked and place into saucepan. Add peas to the potatoes and keep warm over a warm burner until chicken is done. When serving top potatoes and peas with blue cheese and chopped nuts. Cut roasted chicken and set along side of peas and potatoes. Serves 2.

60736D-02

SALMON CAKES WITH CUCUMBER SAUCE

Cucumber Sauce:

1/3 **c. peeled and diced cucumber**   1/8 **tsp. dill**
1/3 **c. plain yogurt**   1/2 **small clove garlic, pressed**

In a small bowl combine all the ingredients. Cover and refrigerate before serving.

Salmon Cakes:

6-oz. can salmon, drained   **1 T. fresh lime juice**
half of 15-oz. can garbanzo beans,   **2 dashes hot sauce**
  drained   1/4 **tsp. ground cumin**
1/2 **c. (about 1 slice) fresh bread**   1/8 **tsp. salt**
  crumbs   **1 egg, beaten slightly**
2 T. chopped black olives   **1 T. cooking oil**

Remove bones and skin from the salmon. Mash garbanzo beans in a medium bowl. Add crumbled salmon, bread crumbs, olives, lime juice, hot sauce, cumin, salt and egg. Stir together well and form 3-inch diameter patties. Heat oil in medium nonstick fry pan. When oil is hot brown salmon patties on both sides and heated through. Serve and top with Cucumber Sauce. Serves 2.

RECIPE FAVORITES

60736D-02

B

reads & Rolls

Favorite Recipes

Helpful Hints

- Over-ripe bananas can be peeled and frozen in a plastic container until it's time to bake bread or cake.

- When baking bread, a small dish of water in the oven will help keep the crust from getting too hard or brown.

- Use shortening, not margarine or oil, to grease pans, as margarine and oil absorb more readily into the dough or batter (especially bread).

- Use a metal ice tray divider to cut biscuits in a hurry. Press into the dough, and biscuits will separate at dividing lines when baked.

- To make self-rising flour, mix 4 cups flour, 2 teaspoons salt, and 2 tablespoons baking powder, and store in a tightly covered container.

- Hot water kills yeast. One way to tell the correct temperature is to pour the water over your forearm. If you cannot feel either hot or cold, the temperature is just right.

- When in doubt, always sift flour before measuring.

- When baking in a glass pan, reduce the oven temperature by 25°.

- When baking bread, you get a finer texture if you use milk. Water makes a coarser bread.

- If your biscuits are dry, it could be from too much handling, or the oven temperature may not have been hot enough.

- Nut breads are better if stored 24 hours before serving.

- To make bread crumbs, toast the heels of bread and chop in a blender or food processor.

- Cracked eggs should not be used because they may contain bacteria.

- The freshness of eggs can be tested by placing them in a large bowl of cold water; if they float, do not use them.

- For a quick, low-fat crunchy topping for muffins, sprinkle the tops with Grape-Nuts cereal before baking.

- Dust a bread pan or work surface with flour by filling an empty glass salt shaker with flour.

Breads & Rolls

HONEY CORNBREAD

⅔ c. flour
⅓ c. cornmeal
1½ tsp. baking powder
¼ tsp. baking soda

¼ c. honey
¼ c. margarine, melted
1 egg, slightly beaten
¼ c. buttermilk

Preheat oven to 425°. Grease 9x5x3-inch loaf pan. In medium bowl stir together flour, cornmeal, baking powder and baking soda. Add honey, margarine, egg and buttermilk. Stir gently until all ingredients are moistened. There will be lumps in the batter. Pour into loaf pan. Bake for 25 minutes. Serve as a side to soups or salads for a complete meal. Makes 1 loaf, serving 6-8.

BANANA NUT BREAD

⅓ c. margarine, softened
⅔ c. sugar
2 eggs, slightly beaten
1 large banana, mashed
1 tsp. vanilla

1⅓ c. flour
1 tsp. baking powder
¼ tsp. baking soda
½ c. buttermilk
⅓ c. chopped pecans or walnuts

Preheat oven to 400°. Grease 9x5x3-inch loaf pan. In medium bowl cream together the margarine and sugar. Add eggs, banana and vanilla. Stir to mix together completely. In separate bowl stir together flour, baking powder and baking soda. Alternately add dry ingredients and buttermilk to bowl of wet ingredients, stirring gently. There should still be some lumps in the batter. Fold in chopped nuts. Do not over mix. Pour batter into greased loaf pan. Bake for 45 min. Makes 1 loaf, serving 6-8.

60736D-02

PUMPKIN (OR APPLESAUCE) SPICE BRAN BREAD

¼ c. + 2 T. All-Bran cereal
2 T. boiling water
1 egg, slightly beaten
3 T. cooking oil
3 T. buttermilk
½ c. canned pumpkin (or thick applesauce)
2 T. sugar
¼ c. brown sugar

¼ tsp. baking soda
¾ tsp. baking powder
½ tsp. cinnamon
⅛ tsp. ground ginger
¼ tsp. nutmeg
⅛ tsp. ground cloves
½ c. + 2 T. flour
3 T. raisins

Preheat oven to 350°. Grease 9X5X3-inch loaf pan. Put All-Bran in medium mixing bowl. Pour boiling water evenly over the cereal and let stand 15 minutes. Stir in egg, cooking oil, buttermilk and pumpkin (or thick applesauce). Once incorporated, stir in sugar and brown sugar. In small bowl stir together baking soda, baking powder, cinnamon, ginger, nutmeg, cloves and flour. Gently stir the dry ingredients into the wet ingredients until evenly moistened. Mixture will be lumpy. Fold in raisins. Pour into loaf pan bake for about 30-35 minutes. Makes 1 loaf, serving 6-8.

BOB'S BUTTERMILK PANCAKES

1 c. flour
½ tsp. baking powder
½ tsp. baking soda
1½ tsp. sugar

1 egg, beaten
1 t. melted butter
1 c. buttermilk

In a medium bowl stir together flour, baking powder, baking soda and sugar. Add egg, melted butter and buttermilk. Stir gently to evenly moisten all dry ingredients. There should still be some small lumps. Do not over mix as this will make pancakes tough. Spoon onto heated nonstick griddle. When bubbles have formed on top and sides look a little dry turn pancakes to brown second side. Makes approx. 8 4-inch pancakes.

60736D-02

CHOCOLATE BANANA BREAD

1 med. very ripe banana	½ c. flour
½ tsp. vanilla	¼ c. cocoa powder
1 egg, slightly beaten	¾ tsp. baking powder
⅓ c. + 2 T. buttermilk	⅛ tsp. baking soda
⅓ c. + 2 T. sugar	½ c. chocolate chips (optional)

Preheat oven to 350°. Grease 9x5x3-inch loaf pan. In a medium bowl mash the banana with a fork. Stir in vanilla, egg, buttermilk and sugar. In a small bowl stir together the flour, cocoa powder, baking powder and baking soda. Then add the dry ingredients to the wet ingredients. If you desire to add chocolate chips add them now. Stir until evenly mixed. Pour into the loaf pan. Bake in 350° oven for 35 minutes until done. Makes 1 loaf, serving 6-8.

DROP BISCUITS

3 T. cooking oil	1 tsp. sugar
1 c. flour + ¼ c. flour	¼ tsp. cream of tartar
2 tsp. baking powder	¾ c. buttermilk
⅛ tsp. baking soda	

Preheat oven to 450°. Pour cooking oil in 9x5x3-inch loaf pan. Put about ¼ c. flour into a small bowl and set aside. In medium bowl stir together 1 c. flour, baking powder, baking soda, sugar and cream of tartar. Gently stir buttermilk into flour mixture just until flour has been incorporated. Mixture will be lumpy. Drop a heaping tablespoonful of dough into the small bowl of flour. Work dough ball with your hands and roll in flour to coat. Compress dough ball to shape into round ball. Drop dough ball into cooking oil in loaf pan. Turn dough ball to coat with oil on all sides. Repeat with remaining dough. Bake for 10-12 minutes or slightly golden brown on top. Makes 6 biscuits.

60736D-02

STUFFED FOCACCIA

1 (1-lb.) frozen loaf of bread
   dough, thawed (or make scratch
   dough for 1 loaf of bread)
1 T. olive oil
1 tsp. basil
¼ tsp. oregano
¼ tsp. marjoram

¼ tsp. rosemary, crushed
⅛ tsp. garlic powder
3 oz. Provolone cheese, sliced
   thin
3 oz. Jarlsberg cheese, sliced thin
2 T. freshly grated Parmesan
   cheese

Preheat oven to 375°. On a floured surface, roll half of the dough into a 5x7-inch rectangle. If dough shrinks back after rolling let it rest 10 minutes. Then try rolling it again. Transfer dough to a greased cookie sheet. Press dough to form a small ridge all the way around the edge. Brush half of the olive oil on the surface of the dough. Sprinkle evenly with basil, oregano, marjoram, rosemary and garlic powder. Cover with Provolone and Jarlsberg cheese slices. On a lightly floured surface, roll the remaining half of the bread dough into a 5x7-inch rectangle. Place it on top of the cheese and herbs. Pinch the edges of the top and bottom crust together. Brush the remaining olive oil on the top and let rise for 30 minutes. Before baking make dimples in the top of the dough by pressing your fingers tips into the dough. Sprinkle dough with Parmesan cheese. Bake 25-30 minutes until golden brown and bread sounds hollow when tapped. Remove from the cookie sheet and cut into rectangular pieces or pie-shaped wedges. Makes 6 servings.

60736D-02

GLAZED BLUEBERRY BISCUITS

Biscuits:

1 c. flour	3 T. margarine, softened
1½ tsp. baking powder	1 egg, beaten
⅛ tsp. baking soda	⅓ c. buttermilk
¼ c. sugar	¼ c. blueberries

Preheat oven to 400°. In a small mixing bowl stir together flour, baking powder, baking soda and sugar. Add margarine and mash with fork to produce small crumbs. Add egg, buttermilk and blueberries. Stir gently until all the ingredients are stuck together. Pour onto a floured surface and knead 4 times. Roll into a small half-inch thick circle. Place on greased cookie sheet. Bake for 15 minutes.

Glaze:

2 T. margarine	⅛ tsp. cinnamon
2 T. sugar	large pinch of nutmeg

Put margarine, sugar, cinnamon and nutmeg in a small cup and heat in microwave oven until margarine is melted. Stir. When biscuits come out of the oven brush or slowly drizzle the margarine mixture over the top of the hot biscuits. Cut into wedges and serve warm. Serves 4.

PESTO-CHEESE FRENCH BREAD

3 T. mayonnaise	¾-1 tsp. pesto
½ small clove garlic, pressed	1 large or 2 small French rolls
3 T. fresh grated Parmesan (or Romano) cheese	

In a small bowl mix together the mayonnaise, garlic and Parmesan (or Romano) cheese and pesto. Cut rolls in two, lengthwise. Spread on cut surface of roll and place under broiler until spread turns a light golden brown. Serves 2.

60736D-02

APPLE-CINNAMON-PECAN BREAKFAST CAKE

Batter:

¼ c. margarine	½ tsp. baking soda
½ c. sugar	½ tsp. cinnamon
2 eggs	½ c. plain yogurt (or sour cream)
1 c. flour	1 c. peeled & chopped apple
½ tsp. baking powder	¼ tsp. vanilla

Preheat oven to 350°. Grease 9x5x3-inch loaf pan. In medium bowl cream together margarine and sugar. Stir in eggs and beat well. In another bowl stir together the flour, baking powder, baking soda and cinnamon. Add to the margarine and sugar mixture. Stir gently until incorporated. Stir in yogurt (or sour cream), apple and vanilla. Set aside.

Topping:

¼ c. + 2 T. brown sugar	1 T. margarine, melted
2 tsp. flour	½ c. chopped walnuts or pecans
¾ tsp. cinnamon	

In a small bowl stir together brown sugar, flour, cinnamon, margarine and nuts. Pour batter into loaf pan. Sprinkle topping over the top. Bake for 25 minutes. Let stand for 10 minutes before cutting to serve. Serves 6-8.

60736D-02

LEMON BREAD

Bread:

1 c. flour	2 eggs
¾ tsp. baking powder	1 T. + 1½ tsp. lemon zest
¾ c. sugar	⅓ c. chopped walnuts or pecans
⅓ c. cooking oil	⅓ c. milk

Preheat oven to 350°. Grease 9x5x3-inch loaf pan. In medium bowl stir together flour, baking powder and sugar. Set aside. In small bowl mix together cooking oil, eggs and lemon zest and beat vigorously for 2 minutes. Stir in milk. Add to the four mixture and gently until all ingredients are incorporated. Fold in chopped nuts. Pour batter into loaf pan. Bake for about 1 hr. 10 minutes.

Lemon Glaze:

¼ c. fresh lemon juice	2 T. sugar

Stir lemon juice and sugar in small bowl until sugar dissolves. When bread is baked and just out of the oven run a knife around edges of bread to loosen it from the pan. Slowly drizzle the glaze over the hot bread allowing glaze to drip down the sides. Cool completely. Turn bread out of pan. Slice to serve. Makes 1 loaf.

60736D-02

BLUEBERRY BRUNCH CAKE WITH LEMON SAUCE

Crumb Topping:

¼ c. sugar
3 T. flour

grated zest of half a lemon
3 T. margarine

Preheat oven to 375°. Grease 9x5x3-inch loaf pan. In small bowl combine sugar, flour and lemon zest. Cut in margarine until coarse crumbs are formed. Set aside.

Cake:

2 c. flour
1½ tsp. baking powder
½ tsp. baking soda
¾ c. sugar
¾ c. + 2 T. buttermilk

2 eggs, beaten
7 T. margarine, melted
1¾ c. fresh or unsweetened
    blueberries

In a large bowl combine the flour, baking powder, baking soda and sugar. Add buttermilk, eggs and melted margarine. Gently stir until well blended. Fold in blueberries. Spoon batter into loaf pan and sprinkle topping over top. Bake for 50 minutes-1 hour or until cake is done. Let cake cool in pan for 15 minutes before serving. Serves 6-8.

Lemon Sauce:

½ c. sugar
1 T. cornstarch
grated zest of 2 lemons

¼ c. fresh lemon juice
¼ c. water
3 T. margarine

In a small saucepan stir to combine the sugar, cornstarch and lemon zest. Add lemon juice and water. Stir while heating over medium heat until boiling. Remove from heat and stir in margarine. Serve the cake in a small pool of lemon sauce. Serves 6.

60736D-02

BASIC BRAN BREAD

1 c. All-Bran cereal	3 T. cooking oil
⅓ c. boiling water	1 tsp. baking soda
1 egg, slightly beaten	⅓ c. sugar
⅔ c. buttermilk	¾ c. + 2 T. flour

Preheat oven to 425°. Grease 9x5x3-inch loaf pan. Put All-Bran cereal in medium mixing bowl with water. Let sit for 10 minutes. Add egg, buttermilk and cooking oil. Stir to incorporate. In separate bowl stir together to blend the baking soda, sugar and flour. Add dry ingredients to the wet ingredients and gently stir to incorporate. Pour into the loaf pan. Bake for 25-30 minutes. Serves 6.

BASIC BRAN BREAD VARIATIONS

Fruit and Nut	Banana
Spicy Applesauce	Blueberry
Chocolate Chip	

When gently stirring the dry ingredients into the wet ingredients of the BASIC BRAN BREAD you may add either of the following ingredients: ⅓ c. raisins, dried sliced apples, dried sliced peaches, or dried sliced bananas and 3 T. chopped pecans or walnuts OR ⅓ c. applesauce, 1 tsp. cinnamon, a pinch of nutmeg, a pinch allspice and reduce cooking oil to 1½ tsp. OR ⅓ c. chocolate chips OR 1 mashed banana and reduce cooking oil to 2 T. OR ⅓ c. fresh or frozen blueberries. Bake as directed in BASIC BRAN BREAD recipe.

60736D-02

CINNAMON-DATE NUT ROLLS

Dough:

2½ **c. flour**	¼ **c. + 2 tsp. milk**
3 **T. sugar**	¼ **c. water**
1 **packet fast-acting dry yeast**	¼ **c. + 2 T. margarine**
½ **tsp. salt**	1 **egg, slightly beaten**

Preheat oven to 375°. Grease 9x5x3-inch loaf pan. Put 1 c. flour, sugar, yeast and salt in medium mixing bowl and stir together. Put milk, water and margarine into a glass measuring cup and heat to 125° in microwave oven. DO NOT OVERHEAT THE LIQUID. If you do, let liquid cool before adding to dry ingredients. Pour into dry ingredients and stir until well incorporated. Add the egg and stir well for 2½ minutes. Slowly add 1¼ c. flour while stirring to incorporate. When a firm dough ball is developed it will pull away from the sides of the bowl. Pour dough onto a well floured, flat surface. Knead 50 times, turning dough a quarter turn each time you knead it. Add more flour if needed to prevent the dough from sticking to the flat surface. Let dough rest 10 minutes while making the filling.

Filling:

½ **c. chopped dates**	2 **tsp. cinnamon**
2 **T. margarine**	⅓ **c. brown sugar**
2 **T. cream cheese**	¼ **c. chopped walnuts or pecans**

In a glass measuring cup put dates and enough water to almost cover. Heat in microwave until fruit is soft. Drain water and discard. Stir in margarine, cream cheese, cinnamon, brown sugar and nuts. To assemble: Using an empty wine bottle as a rolling pin, roll the dough into a 12x16-inch rectangle. Spread the filling completely over the surface of the dough except ½-inch along one 16-inch edge. Start rolling the dough up from the one 16-inch side that has the filling up to the edge to form the traditional cinnamon roll spiral. Moisten the opposite edge of the dough that doesn't have the filling with wet finger tips. Pinch the moistened edge to the dough roll to seal the "seam". Cut the dough crosswise into six equal portions. Place cut side up in loaf pan. To proof rolls, boil 2 c. water in measuring cup in microwave oven to create a steamy oven cavity. Place pan of rolls in microwave with the cup of boiled water and close the door to keep dough warm and moist while proofing. Proof 35-45 minutes or until doubled in size. You may need to remove the dough once during the proofing process to reheat the water to boiling to maintain a warm environment. Then bake for 30-35 minutes. Makes 6 rolls.

60736D-02

BUTTERMILK PANCAKE OR FRYING BATTER MIX

Dry Mix:

¼ c. dry, powdered buttermilk	1 tsp. baking powder
1 c. flour	½ tsp. baking soda
1½ tsp. sugar	

In a medium bowl mix the dry buttermilk, flour, sugar, baking powder and baking soda. Store in sealed glass or plastic container for future use. When ready to use for pancakes or frying batter read the following...

Making Mix Ready To Use:

1 egg, slightly beaten	1½ tsp. margarine, melted
1 c. water	

FOR PANCAKES: When ready to use for pancakes stir gently to incorporate liquid in the dry mix. There should be some small lumps. Do not over mix as this will produce tough pancakes. Makes 8 4-inch pancakes.

FOR FRYING BATTER: To make a frying batter for fish, vegetables or other foods add a little more water to thin the batter. Dip food into the batter and fry in a skillet of hot oil. Cook food completely, turning to brown all sides. Before serving remove and drain on paper towels to absorb excess oil before serving.

60736D-02

ORANGE-RAISIN SCONES WITH ORANGE BUTTER

Scones:

1½ c. flour	¼ c. raisins
1 T. + 1½ tsp. sugar	half of 6-oz. container orange
1 T. baking powder	flavored yogurt
⅛ tsp. baking soda	1 tsp. grated orange zest
3 T. chilled margarine	

Preheat oven to 375°. Grease a 7-inch diameter circle on a cookie sheet. In a small mixing bowl stir together the flour, sugar, baking powder and baking soda. Add margarine in small chunks. Mash the margarine with a fork until it is broken into coarse crumbs. Add raisins, yogurt and orange zest. Stir until mixture begins to hold together. Turn out onto a lightly floured surface. Knead gently 1 minute adding a little more flour when the dough starts to stick to the floured surface. Pat dough into a ½-inch thick round. Cut into 4 wedges and place the wedges on cookie sheet. Bake for about 14 minutes or scones are golden brown. In the meantime, make the Orange Butter below.

Orange Butter:

4 T. butter, softened	¾ tsp. grated orange zest
2 tsp. sugar	

In a cup stir butter, sugar and orange zest until most of the sugar dissolves. Serve with warm scones. Serves 4.

60736D-02

Desserts

Favorite Recipes

_____
_____
_____
_____
_____
_____
_____
_____
_____
_____
_____
_____
_____
_____
_____
_____
_____

Helpful Hints

- Egg whites need to be at room temperature for greater volume when whipped. Remember this when making meringue.

- When preparing several batches of pie dough, roll dough out between sheets of plastic wrap. Stack the discs in a pizza box, and keep the box in the freezer. Pull out the required crusts as needed.

- Place your pie plate on a cake stand when placing the pie dough in it and fluting the edges. The cake stand will make it easier to turn the pie plate, and you won't have to stoop over.

- Many kitchen utensils can be used to make decorative pie edges. For a scalloped edge, use a spoon. Crosshatched and herringbone patterns are achieved with a fork. For a sharply pointed effect, use a can opener to cut out points around the rim.

- Keep strawberries fresh for up to ten days by refrigerating them (unwashed) in an airtight container between layers of paper towels.

- When grating citrus peel, bits of peel are often stuck in the holes of the grater. Rather than waste the peel, you can easily brush it off by using a new, clean toothbrush.

- To core a pear, slice the pear in half lengthwise. Use a melon baller to cut out the central core, using a circular motion. Draw the melon baller to the top of the pear, removing the interior stem as you go.

- When cutting butter into flour for pastry dough, the process is easier if you cut the butter into small pieces before adding it to the flour.

- To keep the cake plate clean while frosting, slide 6-inch strips of waxed paper under each side of the cake. Once the cake is frosted and the frosting is set, pull the strips away leaving a clean plate.

- When decorating a cake with chocolate, you can make a quick decorating tube. Put chocolate in a heat-safe zipper-lock plastic bag. Immerse in simmering water until the chocolate is melted. Snip off the tip of one corner, and squeeze the chocolate out of the bag.

- Professionally decorated cakes have a silky, molten look. To get that appearance, frost your cake as usual, then use a hair dryer to blow-dry the surface until the frosting slightly melts.

- To ensure that you have equal amounts of batter in each pan when making a layered cake, use a kitchen scale to measure the weight.

Desserts

HOT FUDGE DESSERT TOPPING

half of 6-oz. package real
chocolate chips

half of 14-oz. can of evaporated
milk

In medium non-stick saucepan combine chocolate chips and evaporated milk. Cook over medium-low heat stirring constantly until chips are completely melted and well incorporated otherwise the sauce may scorch on the pan bottom. Be patient. Sauce will become thickened. Serve over ice cream, angel food or chocolate cake or brownies. You might dip fresh fruit chunks in the sauce. Makes about ¾ cup.

PEANUT BUTTER-HOT FUDGE TOPPING

½ c. sugar
1 T. flour
1 T. cocoa powder
1 T. water
2 T. peanut butter

one quarter can of 12-oz. can of
evaporated milk
¼ tsp. vanilla
1 T. margarine

In small saucepan stir together the sugar, flour and cocoa powder. Mix thoroughly. Add water to make a paste. Add peanut butter and stir to incorporate. Gradually add evaporated milk and stir until evenly dispersed. Add vanilla and margarine. Heat over medium heat, stirring constantly. When mixture boils remove from heat and cool slightly before serving. Serve over ice cream, brownies or cake. Makes about ¾ cup.

60736D-02

ORANGE DESSERT SAUCE

⅓ c. sugar	1 tsp. margarine
1½ tsp. cornstarch	2 tsp. orange zest
½ c. warm water	¼ c. fresh orange juice

In small saucepan stir together sugar and cornstarch. Pour warm water over the sugar mixture and stir. Stir while cooking over medium-low heat until boiling. Stir in margarine, orange zest and orange juice. Cool slightly and serve over angel food cake, fresh fruit or ice cream. Makes ¾ cup.

GOOEY BROWNIE ICE CREAM BARS

2 squares baking chocolate	¼ tsp. baking powder
5 T. margarine	½ c. walnuts or pecans, chopped
¾ c. sugar	(optional)
2 eggs	ice cream (flavor of your choice)
½ c. + 2 T. flour	

Preheat oven to 350°. Grease a 9x5x3-inch loaf pan. Melt the chocolate and margarine in cup in microwave oven. Pour into a medium bowl with sugar. Mix well. Add eggs and gently stir to incorporate. In a small bowl combine the flour and baking powder. Gently stir the flour mixture and nuts into the chocolate mixture. Be careful not to over mix. Pour into the pan and bake for 30 minutes. The brownies should appear to be under cooked because they will be puffy and dryer around the edges and sunk in the middle. Remove from oven and cool before cutting into 6 or 8 portions. Then cut in half horizontally to make the outer part of the sandwich. Slice ice cream into ½-inch thick slices and place between brownie slices. Serve or freeze for later consumption. Makes 6-8.

60736D-02

LEFTOVER BROWNIE, CAKE OR COOKIE CHOCOLATE PUDDING

¼ c. + 2 T. sugar
1 T. cornstarch
1 c. milk
1 egg, beaten
1 T. margarine

2 squares baking chocolate,
  chopped
¾ tsp. vanilla
½ c. leftover brownies, cake or
  cookies

In a small saucepan combine the sugar and cornstarch. Stir in the milk and egg. Add chocolate chunks and heat over medium-low. Stir constantly to prevent the pudding from sticking while cooking. Cook until pudding just comes to a boil. Remove from the heat and stir in the vanilla. Then stir in the leftover chunks of brownie, cake or cookies. Serves 2-3.

MY FAVORITE APPLE CRISP

3 c. golden delicious apples
  peeled, cored and sliced into
  ⅛-inch pieces
¾ tsp. cinnamon
3 T. water

⅔ c. flour
¾ c. sugar
4 T. margarine
¼ tsp. lemon juice

Preheat oven to 350°. Grease 9x5x3-inch loaf pan. Spread sliced apples evenly over bottom of pan. Sprinkle with cinnamon and water. In a small bowl mix together flour, sugar and margarine until crumbly. Spread over top of apples. Sprinkle with the lemon juice. Bake for 40 minutes until golden brown on top and bubbly. Serves 6.

60736D-02

MRS. T'S APPLE CAKE WITH CREAM CHEESE FROSTING

Cake:

1 egg
³/₄ c. sugar
¹/₃ c. +1 T. cooking oil
³/₄ c. flour
³/₄ tsp. cinnamon

¹/₂ tsp. baking soda
¹/₂ tsp. vanilla
1¹/₂ c. golden delicious apples,
  peeled, cored and diced
¹/₄ c. chopped walnuts or pecans

Preheat oven to 350°. Grease an 9x5x3-inch loaf pan. In large bowl beat eggs and cooking oil until foamy. Mix in sugar. In a medium bowl mix together the flour, cinnamon and baking soda. Stir into the sugar mixture. Then fold in the apples and nuts. Pour into the loaf pan. Bake for 45 minutes.

Cream Cheese Frosting:

2¹/₄ oz. cream cheese, room
  temperature
1 T. melted margarine

¹/₂ tsp. vanilla
¹/₃-¹/₂ c. powdered sugar

Mix all ingredients together in a medium bowl. Spread over cooled cake. Serves 6.

CARROT CAKE

³/₄ c. flour
¹/₂ tsp. baking soda
³/₄ tsp. cinnamon
³/₄ c. sugar
¹/₂ c. + 2 T. cooking oil
1 egg

³/₄ c. finely grated carrots
¹/₃ c. crushed pineapple, well
  drained
¹/₃ c. chopped walnuts or pecans
¹/₂ tsp. vanilla

Preheat oven to 350°. Grease 9x5x3-inch loaf pan. In a small bowl stir the flour, baking soda and cinnamon to blend. In a medium bowl briskly stir together the sugar, oil and egg. Gradually add the flour mixture. Gently stir in the carrots, pineapple, nuts and vanilla. Pour into the loaf pan and bake for 50-55 minutes or until done. Frost with MRS. T'S APPLE CAKE FROSTING. Serves 6.

60736D-02

LEMON CURD

¾ c. water	1 egg
¼ c. fresh lemon juice	4 T. real butter, cut into pieces
⅓ c. + 2 T. sugar	2 tsp. grated lemon rind

Boil water and lemon juice in a small saucepan until reduced to ⅓ cup. Cool some. In a small bowl beat sugar and egg until foamy. Gradually add reduced lemon juice and lemon rind to the egg mixture, stirring as you go. Set bowl over saucepan of boiling water (but not touching the water), stirring constantly. Stir in one piece of butter at a time until melted. Custard will thicken to about the consistency of yogurt (about 12 minutes). DO NOT boil the custard. Serve as a filling in BUTTER POUND CAKE, topping for ice cream or dip for fresh strawberries. Makes about ½ cup.

BUTTER POUND CAKE

1 T. milk	¼ c. sugar
1 egg	¼ tsp. baking powder
½ tsp. vanilla	4 T. butter, melted
½ c. flour	

Preheat oven to 350°. Grease a 2-cup glass or ceramic casserole or soufflé dish. In a small bowl whisk together milk, egg and vanilla. In a medium bowl stir together flour, sugar and baking powder. Add butter to the egg mixture. Pour half of the egg mixture to the flour mixture and stir vigorously with a spoon for 20 seconds. Add remaining egg mixture and stir vigorously for half a minute. Scrape down sides. Pour batter into dish. Bake for 35-40 minutes or until done. Cool 10 minutes before removing from dish. Cool and serve with fresh strawberries and whipped cream. Or you can make a torte by cutting cake into 3 layers and fill with LEMON CURD, softened ice cream, cherry filling, etc. Freeze to set ice cream. Serves 4 or more.

60736D-02

LEMON SPONGE PUDDING

2 T. flour
½ c. sugar
pinch of salt
2 eggs, separated

⅔ c. milk
4 T. fresh lemon juice
1½ T. grated lemon rind
2 tsp. margarine, melted

Preheat oven to 350°. Grease 2-cup casserole or soufflé dish. In a small bowl combine the flour, sugar and salt. In a medium bowl beat eggs until quite foamy. Stir in milk, lemon juice and lemon rind. Add dry ingredients and stir together to form smooth, soupy batter. Stir in melted margarine. Pour batter into casserole or soufflé dish. Place dish in an 8x8-inch baking dish. Add boiling water to 1 inch up side of baking dish. Bake in oven for 35 minutes or top is golden color. Serve hot or room temperature. Serves 2.

CHOCOLATE APPLESAUCE RAISIN CAKE

4 T. margarine
1 c. sugar
1 egg
¾ c. unsweetened applesauce
1¼ c. flour
1 T. baking cocoa

¼ tsp. cinnamon
¼ tsp. cloves
¼ tsp. allspice
½ c. raisins
¼ c. water
1 tsp. baking soda

Preheat oven to 350°. Grease an 8x8-inch baking pan. In a medium bowl cream together the margarine and sugar. Add egg and beat together. Stir in applesauce. Measure flour, cocoa, cinnamon, cloves and allspice in a small bowl and stir to combine. Set aside. Measure raisins in a 1-cup glass measure, add water and heat to near boiling. Stir in the baking soda with the raisins and water (it will bubble momentarily). Stir half the flour mixture into the margarine and sugar mixture. Then stir in half the raisin and water mixture. Repeat until all ingredients are well incorporated. Pour into the pan and bake for 40-45 minutes. Frost with a basic chocolate frosting. Makes 9 servings.

60736D-02

LEMON ICE BOX PIE FOR THREE

Graham Cracker Crust:

8 squares of graham crackers   **2½ T. margarine**

Place graham crackers in a plastic bag and crush by using an empty wine bottle or a rolling pin. Put crumbs and margarine in a 2-cup glass casserole dish. Microwave until margarine is melted. Stir ingredients together until evenly dispersed. Press the mixture onto the bottom and sides of the dish. Cook in microwave oven for 2 minutes. Rotate once during cooking.

Pie Filling and Meringue:

1 egg, separated	**5 drops of vanilla**
1 tsp. sugar	**one third can sweetened**
1 tsp. grated lemon rind	**condensed milk**
juice of 1 lemon	

Preheat oven to 325°. Separate egg and place white in a small mixing bowl. Using a wire whisk beat the egg white with sugar until soft peaks form. Set aside. In medium bowl, beat egg yolk, lemon rind, lemon juice, vanilla and sweetened condensed milk with a wire whisk until well incorporated. Pour into baked pie crust. Top with beaten egg white mixture and bake for 15 minutes or until meringue peaks are golden brown. Chill a couple hours before serving.

BANANA CREAM PIE FOR THREE

graham cracker crust from LEMON ICE BOX PIE FOR THREE	**1 c. milk**
	1 egg, beaten
	1 T. margarine
¼ c. sugar	**¾ tsp. vanilla**
1 T. cornstarch	**½ banana, sliced**

Make graham cracker pie crust in LEMON ICE BOX PIE FOR THREE recipe. In a medium saucepan stir together sugar and cornstarch. Add milk and egg. Heat over medium-low heat just until mixture thickens and comes to a boil. Add margarine and vanilla and stir to incorporate. Lay slices of banana 1 deep in bottom of the prepared pie crust. Pour the cooked pudding over the bananas in the pie crust and refrigerate several hours before serving. Serves 3.

60736D-02

TRIPLE CHOCOLATE PIE FOR THREE

Chocolate Crust:

²/₃ c. chocolate wafer cookie   2½ T. margarine
crumbs

    Place wafer cookies in a plastic bag. Using a wine bottle as a rolling pin crush the chocolate wafers into fine crumbs. Place crumbs and margarine in a 2-cup glass casserole dish. Warm in microwave oven until margarine is melted. Stir to mix the ingredients. Press the mixture onto the bottom and sides of the dish. Microwave 5 minutes.

Pie Filling:

1 oz. cream cheese, softened in   1 egg, beaten
  microwave oven   ⅛ tsp. vanilla
2 tsp. baking cocoa   2 T. chocolate chips
one third can sweetened
  condensed milk

    Preheat oven to 325°. In a medium bowl combine the cream cheese with the baking cocoa. When well incorporated add the sweetened condensed milk, egg and vanilla and beat with whisk. Stir in the chocolate chips. Pour into the wafer crumb crust. Bake for 20 minutes or until set. Serves 3.

60736D-02

BANANA-ORANGE GALETTE

Crust:

1 egg, beaten	1 tsp. grated orange zest
3 T. sugar	1 tsp. vanilla
3 T. cooking oil, butter or	¾ c. flour
softened margarine	⅛ tsp. baking powder

Place egg and sugar in a medium bowl. Using a wire whisk beat until foamy. Stir in cooking oil, orange zest and vanilla. Measure the flour into a 1-cup measure. Stir in baking powder until incorporated. Add to the egg and sugar mixture using a fork to blend. Press dough into a ball. Cover and chill at least an hour.

Filling:

¼ c. raisins	1 tsp. rum (optional)
2 T. orange juice	
1 large or 1½ small bananas,	
sliced into ¼-inch slices	

Preheat oven to 375°. Using a wine bottle as a rolling pin roll the dough on a floured surface into a 10-inch circle. Place on a foil-lined cookie sheet. Combine raisins, orange juice and rum in a 1-cup glass measure. Heat in microwave oven until hot but not boiling. Set aside. Arrange banana slices in overlapping circles on crust, leaving 1 inch border. Drizzle raisin and orange juice mixture over the bananas. Fold up the border over outer edge of bananas. Bake for 20 minutes. Serves 4.

60736D-02

MINI-BAKED ALASKA

4 GAIL'S GRANDMA'S COOKIES
  or MA DOMHOLT'S COOKIES
1 c. ice cream (flavor of your
  choice)

4 egg whites
½ c. sugar

Place cookies on cookie sheet. Top each with a large scoop of ice cream. Freeze for 30 minutes. Beat egg whites until foamy. Gradually add sugar, beating until stiff and shiny. Using a spatula or wide knife spread meringue over the entire surface of the ice cream, being sure to seal the meringue to the edges of the cookie. Freeze another 15 minutes. Preheat oven to 450°. Bake desserts about 5 minutes or until golden brown. Serve immediately. Serves 4.

CREAM CHEESE CAKE FOR THREE

Cheese Cake:

graham cracker crust from
  LEMON ICE BOX PIE FOR
  THREE recipe
4½ oz. cream cheese, softened

⅓ c. sugar
1 egg
½ tsp. vanilla

Preheat oven to 370°. In a small bowl thoroughly mix together the cream cheese, sugar, egg and vanilla. Pour into the baked pie crust. Bake for 15-20 minutes or until set.

Cheese Cake Topping:

⅓ pt. sour cream
1 T. sugar

¼ tsp. vanilla

In a small bowl mix together the sour cream, sugar and vanilla. Pour on top of the baked cheese cake and return it to the oven for 5 minutes. Cool before serving.

60736D-02

Favorite Recipes

Cookies & Candy

Helpful Hints

- Push animal shaped cookie cutters lightly into icing on cakes or cupcakes. Fill depressed outlines with chocolate icing or decorating confections.

- Fill flat bottomed ice cream cones half full with cake batter and bake. Top with icing and decorating confections.

- To make cookie crumbs for your recipes, put cookies into a plastic bag and run a rolling pin back and forth until they are the right size.

- To decorate cookies with chocolate, place cookies on a rack over waxed paper. Dip the tines of a fork with chocolate, and wave the fork gently back and forth making wavy lines.

- A gadget that works well for decorating sugar cookies is an empty plastic thread spool. Simply press the spool into the dough, imprinting a pretty flower design.

- Some holiday cookies require an indent on top to fill with jam or chocolate. Use the rounded end of a honey dipper to make the indent.

- Tin coffee cans make excellent freezer containers for cookies.

- If you only have one cookie sheet on hand, line it with parchment paper. While one batch is baking, load a second sheet of parchment paper to have another batch ready to bake. Cleaning is also easier.

- When a recipe calls for packed brown sugar, fill the correct size measuring cup with the sugar, and then use the next smaller size cup to pack the brown sugar into its cup.

- Dipping strawberries in chocolate? Stick toothpicks into the stem end of the berry. Coat the berries with chocolate, shaking off any excess. Turn the berries upside down and stick the toothpick into a block of styrofoam until the chocolate is set. The finished berries will have chocolate with no flat spots. Another easy solution is to place dipped berries dipped-side up in the holes of an egg carton.

- Cut-up dried fruit sometimes sticks to the blade of your knife. To prevent this problem, coat the blade of your knife with a thin film of vegetable spray before cutting.

- Cutting dessert bars is easier if you score the bars as soon as the pan comes out of the oven. When the bars cool, cut along the scored lines.

Cookies & Candy

GAIL'S GRANDMA'S COOKIES

½ c. margarine	¾ tsp. vanilla
½ c. brown sugar	1½ c. flour
½ c. sugar	¾ tsp. baking soda
2 eggs	⅔ c. chocolate chips

Preheat oven to 350°. Grease cookie sheet. Cream together margarine, brown sugar and sugar. Stir in eggs and vanilla. In a medium bowl mix together the flour and baking soda. Stir into the margarine and sugar mixture. Stir in the chocolate chips. Drop about 2 teaspoonfuls onto the cookie sheet. Bake for about 8-10 minutes until the outer edge of the cookie is soft to the touch but doesn't stick to your finger. The center won't look done. Remove the pan from the oven and let cookies set on the cookie sheet a few minutes before trying to remove. The cookies will continue to cook a little while setting on the cookie sheet. Makes about 32 cookies.

MA DOMHOLT'S COOKIES

½ c. sugar	½ c. Wheaties or corn flakes
½ c. brown sugar	1 c. flour
¾ c. margarine	½ tsp. baking soda
1 egg	½ tsp. baking powder
½ tsp. vanilla	½ c. chopped nuts (optional)
1 c. oatmeal	½ c. coconut

Preheat oven to 350°. Grease cookie sheet. In a medium bowl cream together the sugar, brown sugar and margarine. Stir in egg and vanilla. Mix in oatmeal and cereal. In a small bowl stir together the flour, baking soda and baking powder. Then stir into the oatmeal and sugar mixture. Add nuts and coconut and mix until all ingredients are incorporated. Drop 2 teaspoonfuls onto the cookie sheet. Bake for about 8-10 minutes until the outside edge of the cookie is slightly soft to the touch but doesn't stick to your finger. Remove from the oven and let partially cool on the sheet before removing. Cookies will continue to cook while setting on the cookie sheet. Makes about 36 cookies.

60736D-02

PUMPKIN-NUT SQUARES

Cookie Crust:

½ **c. flour**　　　　　　　¼ **c. brown sugar**
¼ **c. oatmeal**　　　　　　¼ **c. margarine**

Preheat oven to 350°. Grease a 9x5x3-inch loaf pan. Combine flour, oatmeal, brown sugar and margarine in a medium bowl. Mix until crumbly. Press into the loaf pan. Bake for 15 minutes.

Filling:

half of 16-oz. can of pumpkin　　½ **tsp. cinnamon**
half of 12-oz. can evaporated milk　¼ **tsp. ginger**
1 egg　　　　　　　　　　　　　⅛ **tsp. ground cloves**
⅓ **c. sugar**

Combine the the pumpkin, evaporated milk, egg, sugar, cinnamon, ginger and cloves in a medium bowl. Mix well. Pour onto the baked crust and bake for 20 minutes or until filling is beginning to set up.

Topping:

¼ **c. walnuts or pecans, chopped**　　1 **T. margarine**
¼ **c. brown sugar**

Combine the nuts, brown sugar and margarine until crumbly. Sprinkle evenly over the top of the filling. Continue to bake for another 15-20 minutes or until set. Cool. Refrigerate before cutting. Makes 8 bars.

60736D-02

RICH CHOCOLATE BAR COOKIES

¾ c. + 2 T. flour
⅛ tsp. baking soda
2¾ tsp. baking cocoa
½ c. margarine, room temperature
½ c. sugar

½ tsp. vanilla
¼ c. brown sugar
1 egg
½ c. chopped walnuts or pecans
½ c. chocolate chips

Preheat oven to 350°. Grease an 8x8-inch baking pan. Combine flour, baking soda and baking cocoa in a small bowl. Set aside. In a medium bowl cream together the margarine and sugars. Stir in vanilla. Beat in egg. Slowly add the flour mixture. Stir gently just until all ingredients are blended. Stir in nuts and chocolate chips. Pour into the baking pan and spread evenly. Bake for about 25 minutes until light golden brown on top. Makes 16 bars.

CHOCOLATE CHIP-PECAN BARS

Cookie Crust:

6 T. margarine, room temperature   1 c. flour
2 T. + 2 tsp. brown sugar

Preheat oven to 350°. Grease an 8x8-inch baking dish. Beat margarine until fluffy. Gradually add brown sugar. Mix in flour until crumbly. Press into the pan. Bake for 20 minutes.

Topping:

2 T. margarine, melted
2 eggs, slightly beaten
¼ c. corn syrup
3 T. brown sugar

½ tsp. vanilla
½ c. walnuts or pecans, chopped
¾ c. chocolate chips

Combine margarine, eggs, corn syrup, brown sugar and vanilla. Mix well. Stir in nuts and chocolate chips. Pour onto the baked cookie crust. Bake for about 35-40 minutes. Cool before cutting into bars. Makes 16 bars.

60736D-02

MY PEANUT BUTTER COOKIES

½ c. sugar	1 c. peanut butter
4 T. margarine	½ c. + 2 T. flour
1 egg	¼ tsp. baking powder

Preheat oven to 350°. Grease cookie sheet. In a medium bowl cream together sugar and margarine. Mix in egg and peanut butter. In a small bowl stir together flour and baking powder. Slowly stir into the peanut butter mixture. Chill dough. To make cookies roll about 1½ tablespoonfuls of cookie dough between the palms of your hands and place on cookie sheet. Press to slightly flatten. Bake for 10 minutes. Let cool slightly before removing from cookie sheet. Makes about 2 dozen.

MAMO'S DATE BARS

Crust:

½ c. oatmeal	¼ tsp. baking powder
½ c. flour	½ c. brown sugar
½ tsp. baking soda	¼ c. margarine, room temperature

Preheat oven to 350°. Grease a 9x5x3-inch loaf pan. Combine all the ingredients and mix until crumbly. Press ⅔ of the mixture into the bottom of the pan.

Filling:

½ c. chopped dates	¼ c. sugar
½ c. water	

In a 2-cup measuring cup put all the ingredients and bring to a boil in the microwave oven. Stir to combine. Pour on top of the crust and spread to within ¼ inch of the edge. Sprinkle the remaining crust crumbs on top and bake for 30 minutes. Makes 8 bars.

60736D-02

CHOCOLATE-PEANUT BUTTER BARS

Bar Cookie Crust:

¼ **c. margarine**	¼ **tsp. baking soda**
¼ **c. sugar**	¼ **tsp. vanilla**
¼ **c. brown sugar**	½ **c. flour**
1 **egg**	½ **c. oatmeal**
¼ **c. peanut butter**	

Preheat oven to 350°. Grease 9x5x3-inch loaf pan. In a medium bowl cream together margarine, sugar and brown sugar. Mix in egg, peanut butter and vanilla. Stir in flour and oatmeal. Press dough into the bottom of the loaf pan. Bake for 25 minutes or until light, golden brown.

Topping:

half of 6-oz. pkg. chocolate chips	2 **T. peanut butter**
¼ **c. powdered sugar**	1½ **T. water**

When cookie crust is just out of the oven sprinkle the chocolate chips evenly over the top and cover the pan with foil for 5 minutes until the chocolate chips have melted. While the chocolate chips are melting stir together the powdered sugar, peanut butter and water. Then drizzle the peanut butter mixture over the top of the melted chocolate chips and spread the combined toppings over the entire cookie crust using a kitchen knife or spatula. Makes 8 bars.

60736D-02

Recipe Favorites

This & That

Favorite Recipes

_____
_____
_____
_____
_____
_____
_____
_____
_____
_____
_____
_____
_____

Helpful Hints

- To refinish antiques or revitalize wood, use equal parts of linseed oil, white vinegar, and turpentine. Rub into the furniture or wood with a soft cloth and lots of elbow grease.

- To stop the ants in your pantry, seal off cracks where they are entering with putty or petroleum jelly. Also, try sprinkling red pepper on floors and counter tops.

- To fix sticking sliding doors, windows, and drawers, rub wax along their tracks.

- To make a simple polish for copper bottom cookware, mix equal parts of flour and salt with vinegar to create a paste. Store the paste in the refrigerator.

- Applying baking soda on a damp sponge will remove starch deposits from an iron. Make sure the iron is cold and unplugged.

- Remove stale odors in the wash by adding baking soda.

- To clean Teflon™, combine 1 cup water, 2 tablespoons baking soda and ½ cup liquid bleach. Boil in stained pan for 5 to 10 minutes or until the stain disappears. Wash, rinse, dry, and condition with oil before using the pan again.

- Corning Ware can be cleaned by filling it with water and dropping in two denture cleaning tablets. Let stand for 30 to 45 minutes.

- A little instant coffee will work wonders on your wood furniture. Just make a thick paste from instant coffee and a little water, and rub it into the nicks and scratches on your dark wood furniture. You'll be amazed at how new and beautiful those pieces will look.

- For a clogged shower head, boil it for 15 minutes in a mixture of ½ cup vinegar and 1 quart water.

- For a spicy aroma, toss dried orange or lemon rinds into the fireplace.

- Add raw rice to the salt shaker to keep the salt free-flowing.

- Ice cubes will help sharpen garbage disposal blades.

- Separate stuck-together glasses by filling the inside one with cold water and setting them in hot water.

This & That

ORIENTAL MEAT MARINADE

1 med. garlic clove, pressed
1 tsp. fresh ginger, grated
¼ c. cider vinegar or other
   vinegar
¼ c. dry sherry or red wine

½ c. soy sauce
2 T. brown sugar
a pinch of red pepper flakes
   (optional)
½ tsp. sesame oil

Place 1½ lb. beef, pork, fish or poultry in an 8x8-inch baking dish or in a resealable plastic bag. Mix together garlic, ginger, vinegar, sherry, soy sauce, brown sugar, pepper flakes and sesame oil in a 2-cup measuring cup. Pour marinade over top of meat and cover (or seal plastic bag). Place dish (or bag) in refrigerator and let marinate 24 hours. Turn meat at least once during this time. Barbecue, broil or bake to cook. Makes 3 - 4 servings.

CHEF VICKI'S SAUCE FOR PORK OR CHICKEN

1 c. chicken stock
½ c. cream
2 T. dry white wine

¼ tsp. Dijon mustard
¼ tsp. tarragon or sage

Simmer chicken stock, cream, wine, Dijon mustard and herb in a small saucepan. Reduce sauce to ½ to ⅔ cup, stirring frequently. Serve over cooked pork or poultry. Makes ½ to ⅔ cup.

60736D-02

ENCHILADA SAUCE

1 T. + 2 tsp. cooking oil	10½ oz. can tomato purée
1 T. flour	¼ tsp. oregano
1 c. chicken stock	⅛ tsp. cumin
1 T. + 2 tsp. chili powder	1 clove garlic, pressed

In a medium saucepan heat oil. Add flour and stir to incorporate. Slowly stir in chicken stock. Add chili powder, tomato purée, oregano, cumin and garlic. Simmer 15 min. stirring occasionally. Makes 2+ cups.

AL'S FAVORITE BAKED POTATO TOPPING

half of 4 oz.-container plain yogurt	3 T. real bacon bits, finely crumbled
⅓ c. mayonnaise	
1-2 green onion tops, sliced	1 small clove garlic, pressed

Mix yogurt, mayonnaise, onion tops, bacon bits and garlic together in a small bowl. Refrigerate for 3 hours before serving. Serve over hot baked potatoes. Makes 1 cup.

AUNT VERA'S SMOKEY BARBECUE SAUCE

¼ medium onion	2 T. brown sugar
2-3-inch chunk celery stalk	½ tsp. Liquid Smoke
½ c. ketchup	½ tsp. dry mustard
¼ c. cider vinegar	½ tsp. Worcestershire Sauce

Place all ingredients in blender. Blend until ingredients are puréed. Pour into a medium saucepan and simmer for 30 minutes. Pour on top of ribs, chops or browned chicken parts and bake. Or baste on barbecued meat in the last 10 minutes of cooking. Makes about 1¼ c.

60736D-02

SPAGHETTI SAUCE WITH MEAT

½ lb. ground sirloin
½ c. onion, chopped
¼ carrot, diced
¼ stalk celery, diced
2 T. olive oil
2 garlic cloves, pressed
14½-oz. can chopped or diced
   tomatoes in juice

half of 8-oz. can tomato sauce
half of 6-oz. can tomato paste
½ c. dry red wine
2 heaping T. fresh grated
   Parmesan or Romano cheese
1 bay leaf
1 tsp. oregano
1 tsp. basil

Brown ground sirloin with onion, carrot, celery and olive oil in medium sauté pan until onion is clear. Place in crock pot with garlic, tomatoes and the juice, tomato sauce, tomato paste, wine, cheese, bay leaf, oregano and basil. Cook at medium heat for 7-10 hrs. Serve over cooked pasta. Makes 2½ cups.

60736D-02

ORANGE SPICE FRENCH TOAST

Toast:

3 eggs	¼ c. milk or cream
¼ c. orange juice	1 tsp. grated orange zest
3 T. orange liqueur	4-5 slices French bread, cut in
½ tsp. cinnamon	1-inch thick slices
⅛ tsp. coriander	2 T. margarine

The night before you plan to serve the French toast beat the eggs in a medium bowl. Add orange juice, orange liqueur, cinnamon, coriander, milk and orange zest. In an 8x8-inch (or larger if necessary) baking dish place the bread slices so they are a single layer thick. Pour egg mixture over the top. Turn slices to evenly moisten. Cover with plastic wrap and refrigerate overnight. In the morning heat nonstick square griddle. Melt 1 T. margarine on the griddle and spread evenly over the cooking surface. Place slices of soaked bread on the griddle and cook until brown on the one side and turn to brown the other side. Use more margarine on griddle for flavor and to reduce sticking. Serves 2.

Rum Syrup:

½ c. real maple syrup	1 T. dark rum
½ c. honey	

Put all ingredients into a measuring cup and warm in microwave oven before serving.

60736D-02

BREAKFAST CASSEROLE

6-8 oz. ground breakfast sausage
¼ c. chopped onion
3 eggs
¾ c. milk
¾ tsp. dry mustard

salt and pepper
3 slices white bread
¼ c. shredded Jack cheese
¼ c. shredded cheddar cheese

Start preparation the night before you plan to serve the casserole. Grease an 9x5x3-inch loaf pan. Cook the sausage and onion in a medium fry pan. Drain on a paper towel. In a medium bowl beat together the eggs, milk, mustard, salt and pepper. Place the bread slices in the bottom of the loaf pan. Top with the cooked sausage and cheeses. Pour the egg mixture over the top and cover the dish with plastic wrap. Refrigerate overnight. In the morning preheat oven to 350°. Remove the plastic wrap and bake casserole for about 30 minutes. Serves 2.

ASPARAGUS STRATA

1½ tsp. margarine
2 c. sliced asparagus, cut in
  1-inch lengths
⅓ c. diced onion
3 T. water
¼ tsp. tarragon

½ tsp. grated lemon rind
salt and pepper
4 slices sourdough bread
⅔ c. shredded Asiago cheese
1¼ c. milk
4 eggs

Prepare strata the night before you intend to serve it. Grease a 9x5x3-inch loaf pan. Melt margarine in medium nonstick fry pan over medium heat. Add asparagus, onion and water. Bring to a boil, cover and reduce heat so asparagus simmers for 10 minutes. Remove from heat and drain. Stir in tarragon, lemon rind, salt and pepper. Arrange two of the bread slices in a single layer in the bottom of the loaf pan. Top slices with half the asparagus mixture and sprinkle with half the cheese. Repeat the procedure using the remaining bread, asparagus mixture and cheese. In a medium bowl whisk together the milk and eggs. Pour over the strata. Cover with plastic wrap and refrigerate overnight. In the morning preheat the oven to 400°. Remove the wrap and bake for 35 minutes or until golden on top and set. Serves 4.

60736D-02

TURKEY WRAPS

half of 3-oz. package cream
   cheese, softened
2 T. salsa
2 8-inch flour tortillas
1 c. shredded lettuce

1½ c. shredded turkey (or
   chicken) meat
2 green onions, sliced
2 T. cilantro, chopped
3 T. chopped black olives

Mix together the cream cheese and salsa until smooth. Spread half of mixture on each tortilla. Spoon half of the remaining ingredients on top of each tortilla. Roll tortilla to enclose the filling. Serves 2.

SMOKED SALMON ROLL-UP

half of 3-oz. package of cream
   cheese, softened
2-3 drops liquid smoke
½ of small clove garlic, pressed
1 T. fresh chopped parsley

1 c. cooked salmon, flaked
2 8-inch flour tortillas
⅓ c. chopped cucumber
1 thin slice red onion
2 tsp. capers

In a medium bowl mix together the cream cheese, liquid smoke and garlic. Add parsley and salmon, mix well. Spread half the salmon mixture on each tortilla. Sprinkle with half of cucumber, onion and capers. Roll tortilla to enclose filling. Serves 2.

CAESAR SALAD SANDWICH

2 kaiser rolls
1-2 cooked chicken breasts,
   sliced thin
1 small tomato, sliced
2 leaves of romaine lettuce

3 T. BONE'S RESTAURANT'S
   CAESAR SALAD DRESSING
2 T. fresh shredded Parmesan or
   Romano cheese

Slice the rolls in half horizontally and remove some of the soft interior. Reserve the interior for use as bread crumbs in another recipe. On the bottom of the roll lay the chicken and tomato slices. Set the lettuce on top. On the roll top spread a generous amount of Caesar dressing and sprinkle with cheese. Put the halves together and enjoy. Serves 2.

60736D-02

CHICKEN PITA WITH PECAN CREAM CHEESE

2 T. cream cheese, softened
⅛ tsp. thyme
½ of celery stalk, minced
½ of small garlic clove, pressed
2 T. finely chopped walnuts or
  pecans

½ of pear or apple, diced
2 pitas, cut in half to form pockets
1½ c. cooked chicken meat,
  pulled or sliced thin
2 romaine lettuce leaves

In a small bowl mix together cream cheese, thyme, celery, garlic, nuts and fruit. Spread inside the pita pockets. Then lay the chicken and lettuce in the pockets. Serves 2.

RECIPE FAVORITES

Recipe Favorites

60736D-02

INDEX OF RECIPES

WORLD FAMOUS
RESTAURANT'S SHRIMP
SPECIALTY   45

Breads & Rolls

Desserts

Cookies & Candy

This & That

INGREDIENT INDEX

Fruits

Citrus-Chicken Salad	19
Pea Salad	19
A Famous Restaurant's Salad Dressing	22
Bone's Restaurant Caesar Salad Dressing	22
Curried Sauce For Broccoli Or Cauliflower	27
Sautéed Yams With Lemon & Thyme	29
Steamed Broccoli With Lemon Butter	30
Oriental Asparagus	35
Sloppy Joes	39
Chicken Divan	39
World Famous Restaurant's Shrimp Specialty	45
Baked Fish With Horseradish Cream Sauce	47
Artichoke And Lemon Pasta	51
Pork Chops In Orange Sauce	55
Roasted Chicken With Garlic Mayonnaise	61
Chicken With Tarragon Cream Sauce	62
Chicken In Chutney Cream Sauce	64
Scallops In Wine And Butter Sauce	65
Chicken Piccata	68
Lemon Bread	79
Blueberry Brunch Cake With Lemon Sauce	80
My Favorite Apple Crisp	87
Lemon Curd	89
Lemon Sponge Pudding	90
Lemon Ice Box Pie For Three	91
Asparagus Strata	105

Limes-

Crab Meat Spread	3
Fruit Juice Or Wine Cooler	4
Cocktail Sauce For Shrimp Or Crab	5
Black Bean Soup	10
Thai-Style Shrimp Bisque	13
Dressing For Fresh Fruit Salad	15
Salmon With Lime-Thyme Mayonnaise	47
Broiled Or Barbecued Prawns With Lime Butter	49
Salmon On A Bed Of Greens With Lime-Ginger Dressing	51
Fajitas	52
Pork Or Chicken Quesadillas	53
Margarita Chicken Breasts	58
Spicy Peanut Chicken	60
Indian Spiced Chicken Breasts	61
Singapore Chicken	63
Chicken And Pineapple Kabobs	63
Salmon Cakes With Cucumber Sauce	72

Oranges-

Fruit Juice Or Wine Cooler	4
Lemony Fruit Salad	15
Orange And Red Onion Salad	16
Orange-Avocado Salad	17
Citrus Chicken Salad	18
Ginger-Marmalade Yams	27
Fettuccini Alfredo	28
Rice Pilaf	28
Gorgonzola Au Gratin Potatoes	31
Shrimp In Orange-Thyme Sauce	49
Pork Chops in Orange Sauce	55
Singapore Chicken	63
Orange–Raisin Scones With Orange Butter	84
Orange Dessert Sauce	86
Banana-Orange Galette	93
Orange Spice French Toast	104

Strawberries-

Spinach And Strawberry Salad	18

Vegetables

Asparagus-

Great Asparagus	32
Oriental Asparagus	35
Asparagus And Penne	65
Asparagus Strata	105

Avocados-

Orange-Avocado Salad	17
Taco Salad	21
Mix And Match Salad Or Sandwich	23
Fajitas	52
Al's Favorite Chicken-Avocado Sandwich	62

Bell Peppers-

Fish Gumbo	9
Cream Of Potato Soup	14
Citrus-Chicken Salad	19
Rice-A-Roni Salad For A Crowd	21
Mix And Match Salad Or Sandwich	23
Kay's Pizza Request	40
Chicken And Pineapple Kabobs	63

Broccoli-

Cream Of Broccoli Soup	12
Broccoli Salad	22
Curried Sauce For Broccoli or Cauliflower	27
Steamed Broccoli With Lemon Butter	30
Broccoli And Rice Casserole	32
Chicken Divan	39

Cabbage-

Minestrone Soup	7
Holiday Cabbage	30

Carrots-

Split Pea Soup	7
Lemon-Chicken Soup	10
Chicken Bisque	24
Tarragon Buttered Carrots	34
Beef Bourguignon	45
Shepherd's Pie With Garlic Mashed Potato Top	69
Carrot Cake	88
Spaghetti Sauce With Meat	103

Cauliflower-

Cream Of Cauliflower Soup	11
Curried Sauce For Broccoli Or Cauliflower	27

Celery-

Minestrone Soup	7
Split Pea Soup	7
Fish Gumbo	9
Easy Beanless Chili	9
Lemon-Chicken Soup	10
Cream of Broccoli Soup	12
Thai-Style Shrimp Bisque	13
Cream Of Potato Soup	14
Citrus-Chicken Salad	19
Too Good To Pass Up Tomato-Shrimp Aspic	20
Chicken Bisque	24
Dill-Chicken Salad	25
Broccoli And Rice Casserole	32
Sloppy Joes	39
Chicken Gumbo	43
Southern Chicken And Dumplings	46
Aunt Vera's Smokey Barbecue Sauce	102
Spaghetti Sauce With Meat	103
Chicken Pita With Pecan Cream Cheese	107

Cilantro-

Thai-Style Shrimp Bisque	13
Mix And Match Salad Or Sandwich	23
Mexican Chicken Soup	24
Pork Or Chicken Quesadillas	53
Turkey Wraps	106

Cucumbers-

Zingy Cucumber Chips	2
Black Bean Soup	10
Orange-Avocado Salad	17
Mix And Match Salad Or Sandwich	23
Salmon On A Bed Of Greens With Lime-Ginger Dressing	51
Salmon Cakes With Cucumber Sauce	72
Smoked Salmon Roll-Up	106

Green Onions-

Smoked Salmon Cheese Spread	3
Bacon-Cheese Spread With Chutney Or Preserves	6
Orange-Avocado Salad	17
Greek Salad	17
Citrus-Chicken Salad	19
Pea Salad	19
Rice-A-Roni Salad For A Crowd	20
Too Good To Pass Up Tomato-Shrimp Aspic	20
Broiled Or Barbequed Prawns With Lime Butter	49
Artichoke And Lemon Pasta	51
Pecan Encrusted Pork Tenderloin With Garlic-Ginger Mayonnaise	56
Spicy Peanut Chicken	60
Al's Favorite Chicken-Avocado Sandwich	62
Al's Favorite Baked Potato Topping	102

Ginger (fresh)-

Lentil Soup	8
Thai-Style Shrimp Bisque	13
Ginger-Marmalade Yams	27
Mashed Yams With Garlic And Ginger	29
Salmon On A Bed Of Greens With Lime-Ginger Dressing	51
Oriental Halibut	48
Pecan Encrusted Pork Tenderloin With Garlic-Ginger Mayonnaise	56
Spicy Peanut Chicken	60
Indian Spiced Chicken Breasts	61
Singapore Chicken	63
Chicken And Pineapple Kabobs	63

| Chicken In Chutney Cream Sauce | 64 |
| Oriental Meat Marinade | 101 |

Mushrooms-

Orange-Avocado Salad	17
Rice Pilaf	28
Sausage Cream Pasta	37
Stroganoff For Two	37
Easy Lasagne	38
Kay's Pizza Request	40
Chicken Cacciatore	42
Beef Bourguignon	45
Creamy Beef And Tomato Casserole	50
Pork Medallions With Mushrooms	58
Dieter's Delight Chicken Breast	59
Chicken To Die For	60
Al's Favorite Chicken-Avocado Sandwich	62

Peas-

Pea Salad	19
Chicken-Asiago With Orzo	43
Mustard Vinaigrette Roasted Chicken And Potato Salad	71

Potatoes-

Fish Chowder	11
Cream Of Potato Soup	14
Hot German Potato Salad	18
Gorgonzola Au Gratin Potatoes	31
Brandied Yam And Potato Au Gratin	32
Potato And Sweet Onion Packets	35
Roasted Yams And Potatoes	35
Hash Brown And Cheese Potatoes	36
Chicken-Artichoke Hash	44
Chicken With Bacon And Potatoes	64
Shepherd's Pie With Garlic Mashed Potato Top	69
Mustard Vinaigrette Roasted Chicken And Potato Salad	71

Spinach-

Spinach And Strawberry Salad	18
Mix And Match Salad Or Sandwich	23
Dill-Chicken Salad	25
Italian Chicken	66
Spinach-Ricotta Stuffed Pasta Shells	70

Tomatoes-

| Pea Salad | 19 |
| Taco Salad | 21 |

60736-pw   9.6.e.

Mix And Match Salad Or Sandwich	23
Shrimp-Feta-Tomato Pasta	44
Soft Tacos	50
Fajitas	52
Pork Or Chicken Quesadillas	53
Asparagus And Penne	65
Italian Chicken	66
Caesar Chicken Sandwich	106

Sun Dried Tomatoes-
Sausage Cream Pasta	37
Artichoke And Lemon Pasta	51
Roasted Chicken With Garlic Mayonnaise	61
Spinach-Ricotta Stuffed Pasta Shells	70

Yams-
Ginger-Marmalade Yams	27
Mashed Yams With Garlic And Ginger	29
Sautéed Yams With Lemon And Thyme	29
Brandied Yam And Potato Au Gratin	32
Roasted Yams And Potatoes	35

Zucchini-
Minestrone Soup	7
Mix And Match Salad Or Sandwich	23
Au Gratin Zucchini	29
Spiced Summer Squash	33
Special Zucchini	33
Grilled Zucchini	34
Stuffed Zucchini	67

Canned Goods

Applesauce-
Pumpkin (Or Applesauce) Spice Bran Bread	74
Basic Bran Bread Variations	81
Chocolate Applesauce Raisin Cake	90

Artichoke Hearts-
Hot Artichoke Spread	1
Chicken-Artichoke Hash	44
Artichoke And Lemon Pasta	51
Roasted Chicken With Garlic Mayonnaise	61
Feta And Artichoke Stuffed Chicken Pockets	66

Coconut Milk-
Thai-Style Shrimp Bisque   13
Oriental Halibut   48

Garbanzo Beans-
Skinny Greek Bean Spread   2
Salmon Cakes With Cucumber Sauce   72

Marinated Artichoke Hearts-
Greek Salad   17
Rice-A-Roni Salad For A Crowd   21

Pineapple-
Kay's Pizza Request   40
Oriental Halibut   48
Chicken And Pineapple Kabobs   63
Carrot Cake   88

Pumpkin-
Pumpkin Or Applesauce Spice Bran Bread   74
Pumpkin-Nut Squares   96

Beef Consume-
My French Onion Soup   8
Rice Pilaf   28

Beef Stock-
Minestrone Soup   7
My French Onion Soup   8
Beef Bourguignon   45
Pork Chops Smothered In Caramelized Onions   55
Shepherd's Pie With Garlic-Mashed Potato Top   69

Chicken Stock-
My French Onion Soup   8
Fish Gumbo   9
Black Bean Soup   10
Lemon-Chicken Soup   10
Fish Chowder   11
Cream Of Cauliflower Soup   11
Cream Of Broccoli Soup   12
Fettuccini Alfredo   28
Brandied Yam And Potato Au Gratin   32
Mexican Casserole   38
Mediterranean Chicken Dinner   42

Chicken-Asiago With Orzo	43
Shrimp-Feta-Tomato Pasta	44
Robin's Favorite	46
Baked Fish With Horseradish Cream Sauce	47
Artichoke And Lemon Pasta	51
German Sour Cream And Dill Pork Chops	54
Pork Cutlets With Creamy Sage Sauce	57
Pork Medallions With Mushrooms	58
Spicy Peanut Chicken	60
Chicken In Chutney Cream Sauce	64
Chicken With Bacon And Potatoes	64
Chef Vicki's Sauce For Pork Or Chicken	101
Enchilada Sauce	102

Cream Of Mushroom or Cream Of Chicken Soup Concentrate-

Curried Sauce For Broccoli Or Cauliflower	27
Broccoli And Rice Casserole	32
Hash Brown And Cheese Potatoes	36
Mexican Casserole	38
Chicken Divan	39
Tuna Casserole	41

Tomatoes-

Minestrone	7
Easy Beanless Chili	9
Cream Of Tomato Soup	12
Mexican Chicken Soup	24
Mediterranean Chicken Dinner	42
Chicken Cacciatore	42
Robin's Favorite	46
Spaghetti Sauce With Meat	103

Tomato Paste-

Thai-Style Shrimp Bisque	13
Kay's Pizza Request	40
Beef Bourguignon	45
Spaghetti Sauce With Meat	103

Tomato Sauce-

Easy Beanless Chili	9
Sloppy Joes	39
Kay's Pizza Request	40
Chicken Cacciatore	42
Creamy Beef And Tomato Casserole	50
Grampy's Meatloaf	56
Spaghetti Sauce With Meat	103

Meat & Fish

Bacon-

Bacon-Cheese Spread With Chutney Or Preserves	6
Minestrone Soup	7
Fish Gumbo	9
Fish Chowder	11
Cream Of Potato Soup	14
Hot German Potato Salad	18
Pea Salad	19
Broccoli Salad	22
Mix And Match Salad Or Sandwich	23
Special Zucchini	**33**
Mediterranean Chicken Dinner	42
Beef Bourguignon	45
Chicken To Die For	60
Chicken With Bacon And Potatoes	64
Devonshire Sandwiches	67
Al's Favorite Baked Potato Topping	102

Fish or Salmon-

Smoked Salmon Cheese Spread	3
Fish Gumbo	9
Fish Chowder	11
Mix And Match Salad Or Sandwich	23
Salmon Cakes With Cucumber Sauce	72
Salmon With Lime-Thyme Mayonnaise	47
Baked Fish With Horseradish Cream Sauce	47
Oriental Halibut	48
Salmon On A Bed Of Greens With Lime -Ginger Dressing	51
Smoked Salmon Roll-Up	106

Ham-

Lentil Soup	8
Mix And Match Salad Or Sandwich	23
Spinach-Ricotta Stuffed Pasta Shells	70

Sausage-

Split Pea Soup	7
Lentil Soup	8
Fish Gumbo	9
Sausage Cream Pasta	37
Kay's Pizza Request	40
Chicken Gumbo	43
Stuffed Zucchini	67
Shepherd's Pie With Garlic-Mashed Potato Top	69

Spinach-Ricotta Stuffed Pasta Shells	70
Breakfast Casserole	105

Shrimp or Prawns-

Thai-Style Shrimp Bisque	13
Too Good To Pass Up Tomato-Shrimp Aspic	20
Shrimp-Feta-Tomato Pasta	44
World Famous Restaurant's Shrimp Specialty	45
Broiled Or Barbecued Prawns With Lime Butter	49
Shrimp In Orange-Thyme Sauce	49

Condiments

Capers-

Mix And Match Salad Or Sandwich	23
Pork Medallions With Mushrooms	58
Dieter's Delight Chicken Breast	59
Chicken In Tarragon Cream Sauce	62
Chicken Piccata	68
Smoked Salmon Roll-Ups	106

Chutney, Mango-

Easy Chutney Cheese Ball	5
Bacon Cheese Spread with Chutney or Berry Preserves	6
Mix And Match Salad & Sandwich	23
Singapore Chicken	63
Chicken In Chutney Cream Sauce	64

Horseradish-

Smoked Salmon Cheese Spread	3
Cocktail Sauce For Shrimp Or Crab	5
Mix And Match Salad Or Sandwich	23
Baked Fish with Horseradish Cream Sauce	47

Olives, Black-

Fabulous Blue Cheese Spread	1
Smoked Salmon Cheese Spread	3
Mix And Match Salad Or Sandwich	23
Mexican Chicken Soup	24
Easy Lasagne	38
Mexican Casserole	38
Kay's Pizza Request	40
Kay's Pizza Request	40
Salmon Cakes With Cucumber	72
Pork Or Chicken Quesadillas	53
Turkey Wraps	106

Olives, Greek (Kalamata)-

Greek Olive And Garlic Spread	5
Greek Salad	17
Mix And Match Salad Or Sandwich	23
Mediterranean Chicken Dinner	42
Robin's Favorite	46
Chicken To Die For	60

Olives, Stuffed Green-

Rice-A-Roni Salad For A Crowd	20
Too Good To Pass Up Tomato-Shrimp Aspic	20
Mix And Match Salad Or Sandwich	23

Baking Supplies, Nuts & Seeds
Chocolate Chips-

Chocolate Banana Bread	75
Basic Bran Bread Variations	81
Hot Fudge Dessert Topping	85
Triple Chocolate Pie For Three	92
Gail's Grandma's Cookies	95
Rich Chocolate Bar Cookies	97
Chocolate Chip Pecan Bars	97
Chocolate-Peanut Butter Bars	99

Milk, Evaporated-

Fish Chowder	11
Hot Fudge Dessert Topping	85
Peanut Butter-Hot Fudge Topping	85
Pumpkin-Nut Squares	96

Milk, Sweetened Condensed-

Lemon Ice Box Pie For Three	91
Triple Chocolate Pie For Three	92

Peanuts, Cashews or Almonds-

Orange-Avocado Salad	17
Spinach And Strawberry Salad	18
Mix And Match Salad Or Sandwich	23
Dill-Chicken Salad	25

Sesame Seeds or Sunflower Seeds-

Broccoli Salad	22
Mix And Match Salad Or Sandwich	23
Oriental Asparagus	35
Singapore Chicken	63

Walnuts or Pecans-

Fabulous Blue Cheese Spread	1
Smoked Salmon Cheese Spread	3
Bacon-Cheese Spread With Chutney or Berry Preserves	6
Easy Chutney Cheese Ball	5
My Salad Creation	20
Mix And Match Salad Or Sandwich	23
Oriental Halibut	48
Pecan Encrusted Pork Tenderloin With Garlic-Ginger Mayonnaise	56
Mustard Vinaigrette Roasted Chicken And Potato Salad	71
Banana Nut Bread	73
Apple-Cinnamon-Pecan Breakfast Cake	78
Lemon Bread	79
Basic Bran Bread Variations	81
Mrs. T's Apple Cake With Cream Cheese Frosting	88
Carrot Cake	88
Cinnamon-Date Nut Rolls	82
Gooey Brownie Ice Cream Bars	86
Ma Domholt's Cookies	95
Pumpkin-Nut Squares	96
Rich Chocolate Bar Cookies	97
Chocolate Chip Pecan Bars	97
Chicken Pita With Pecan Cream Cheese	107

Fast-Rising Yeast-

Kay's Pizza Request	40
Stuffed Focaccia	76
Cinnamon-Date Nut Rolls	82

Dairy Products

Buttermilk-

Blue Cheese Dressing	15
Honey Cornbread	73
Banana Nut Bread	73
Pumpkin Or Applesauce Spice Bran Bread	74
Bob's Buttermilk Pancakes	74
Chocolate Banana Bread	75
Drop Biscuits	75
Glazed Blueberry Biscuits	77
Blueberry Brunch Cake With Lemon Sauce	80
Basic Bran Bread	81

Cheese, Asiago-

Mix And Match Salad Or Sandwich	23
Chicken-Asiago With Orzo	43
Asparagus Strata	105

Cheese, Blue-

Fabulous Blue Cheese Spread	1
Blue Cheese Dressing	15
My Salad Creation	20
Mix And Match Salad Or Sandwich	23
Mustard Vinaigrette Roasted Chicken And Potato Salad	71

Cheese, Cottage-

Creamy Beef And Tomato Casserole	50

Cheese, Cheddar-

Bacon-Cheese Spread With Chutney Or Berry Preserves	6
Cream Of Cauliflower Soup	11
Taco Salad	21
Mix And Match Salad Or Sandwich	23
Scalloped Eggplant	31
Great Asparagus	32
Brandied Yams And Potato Au Gratin	32
Broccoli And Rice Casserole	32
Hash Browns And Cheese Potatoes	36
Mexican Casserole	38
Easy Lasagne	38
Chicken Divan	39
Kay's Pizza Request	40
Tuna Casserole	41
Soft Tacos	50
Pork Or Chicken Quesadillas	53
Al's Favorite Chicken-Avocado Sandwich	62
Stuffed Zucchini	67
Breakfast Casserole	105

Cheese, Cream-

Fabulous Blue Cheese Spread	1
Salsa And Cream Cheese Dip	1
Hot Artichoke Spread	1
Crab Meat Spread	3
Smoked Salmon Cheese Spread	3
Easy Chutney Cheese Ball	5
Mix And Match Salad Or Sandwich	23
Dill-Chicken Salad	25
Stroganoff For Two	37
Creamy Beef And Tomato Casserole	50
Italian Chicken	66
Cinnamon-Date Nut Rolls	82
Mrs. T's Apple Cake With Cream Cheese Frosting	88
Triple Chocolate Pie For Three	92

Cream Cheese Cake For Three   94
Turkey Wraps   106
Smoked Salmon Roll-up   106
Chicken Pita With Pecan Cream Cheese   107

Cheese, Feta-
Greek Salad   17
Mix And Match Salad Or Sandwich   23
Shrimp-Feta-Tomato Pasta   44
Feta And Artichoke Stuffed Chicken Pockets   66

Cheese, Gorgonzola-
Blue Cheese Dressing   15
My Salad Creation   20
Mix And Match Salad Or Sandwich   23
Gorgonzola Au Gratin Potatoes   31

Cheese, Gouda-
Mix And Match Salad Or Sandwich   23
Pork Chops Smothered In Caramelized Onions   55

Cheese, Havarti-
Robin's Favorite   46
Havarti Stuffed Chicken Breasts   65

Cheese, Mozzarella-
Mix And Match Salad Or Sandwich   23
Easy Lasagne   38
Kay's Pizza Request   40
Pork Or Chicken Quesadillas   53
Italian Chicken   66

Cheese (Parmesan or Romano)-
Hot Artichoke Spread   1
Minestrone Soup   7
Cream Of Broccoli Soup   12
Bone's Restaurant Caesar Salad Dressing   22
Fettuccini Alfredo   28
Au Gratin Zucchini   29
Brandied Yams And Potatoes Au Gratin   32
Chicken-Artichoke Hash   44
Robin's Favorite   46
Parmesan Baked Chicken   59
Asparagus And Penne   65
Italian Chicken   66
Feta And Artichoke Stuffed Chicken Pockets   66
Devonshire Sandwiches   67

Stuffed Zucchini	67
Spinach-Ricotta Stuffed Pasta Shells	70
Stuffed Focaccia	76
Pesto-Cheese French Bread	77
Spaghetti Sauce With Meat	103
Caesar Salad Sandwich	106

Cheese, Ricotta-
| Pork Or Chicken Quesadillas | 53 |
| Spinach-Ricotta Stuffed Pasta Shells | 70 |

Cream-
Lemon-Chicken Soup	10
Cream Of Broccoli Soup	12
Fettuccini Alfredo	28
Au Gratin Zucchini	29
Sausage Cream Pasta	37
Chicken-Artichoke Hash	44
Baked Fish With Horseradish Cream Sauce	47
Shrimp In Orange-Thyme Sauce	49
Artichoke And Lemon Pasta	51
Pork Tenderloin With Apple And Brandy Sauce	57
Chicken To Die For	60
Chicken With Tarragon Cream Sauce	62
Chicken In Chutney Cream Sauce	64
Chef Vicki's Sauce For Pork And Chicken	101
Orange Spice French Toast	104

Sour Cream-
Hot Artichoke Spread	1
Crab Meat Spread	3
Lentil Soup	8
Black Bean Soup	10
Cream Of Cauliflower Soup	11
Blue Cheese Dressing	15
Citrus-Chicken Salad	19
Pea Salad	19
Dill-Chicken Salad	25
Fettuccini Alfredo	28
Hash Brown And Cheese Potatoes	36
Stroganoff For Two	37
Mexican Casserole	38
Chicken Smothered In Mustard-Dill Sauce Over Rice	48
Creamy Beef And Tomato Casserole	50
Fajitas	52
Pork Or Chicken Quesadillas	53

German Sour Cream And Dill Pork Chops	54
Apple-Cinnamon-Pecan Breakfast Cake	78
Cream Cheese Cake For Three	94

Yogurt, Plain-
Indian Spiced Chicken Breasts	61
Salmon Cakes With Cucumber Sauce	72
Apple-Cinnamon-Pecan Breakfast Cake	78
Al's Favorite Baked Potato Topping	102

Miscellaneous

Eggs, Pasteurized-
A Famous Restaurant's Salad Dressing	22
Bone's Restaurant Caesar Salad Dressing	22
Salmon With Lime-Thyme Mayonnaise	47
Pecan Encrusted Pork Tenderloin With Garlic-Ginger Mayonnaise	56

Pita Bread-
Skinny Greek Bean Spread	2
Mix And Match Salad Or Sandwich	23
Chicken Pita With Pecan Cream Cheese	107

Rum-
Hot Buttered Rum Batter	4
Baked Acorn Squash	33
Orange Spice French Toast	104

Sesame Oil-
Skinny Greek Bean Spread	2
Spinach And Strawberry Salad	18
Oriental Asparagus	35
Oriental Halibut	48
Pecan Encrusted Pork Tenderloin With Garlic-Ginger Mayonnaise	56
Chicken And Pineapple Kabobs	63
Singapore Chicken	63
Oriental Meat Marinade	101

Tequila-
Killer Margaritas	4
Fajitas	52
Margarita Chicken Breasts	58

Tortillas-
Mix And Match Salad Or Sandwich	23

Soft Tacos	50
Fajitas	52
Pork Or Chicken Quesadillas	53
Smoked Salmon Roll-Up	106
Turkey Wraps	106

Wine, Sherry, Vermouth or Brandy-

Fruit Juice Or Wine Cooler	4
My French Onion Soup	8
Thai-Style Shrimp Bisque	13
Ginger-Marmalade Yams	27
Fettuccini Alfredo	28
Holiday Cabbage	30
Brandied Yam And Potato Au Gratin	37
Stroganoff For Two	37
Mediterranean Chicken Dinner	42
Chicken Cacciatore	42
Chicken Gumbo	43
Shrimp-Feta-Tomato Pasta	44
Beef Bourguignon	45
World Famous Restaurant's Shrimp Specialty	45
Baked Fish With Horseradish Cream Sauce	47
Broiled Or Barbequed Prawns With Lime Butter	49
Artichoke And Lemon Pasta	51
Pork Tenderloin With Apple And Brandy Sauce	57
Pork Medallions With Mushrooms	58
Parmesan Baked Chicken	59
Scallops In Wine And Butter Sauce	65
Oriental Meat Marinade	101
Chef Vicki's Sauce For Pork Or Chicken	101
Spaghetti Sauce With Meat	103

PANTRY BASICS

A WELL-STOCKED PANTRY provides all the makings for a good meal. With the right ingredients, you can quickly create a variety of satisfying, delicious meals for family or guests. Keeping these items in stock also means avoiding extra trips to the grocery store, saving you time and money. Although everyone's pantry is different, there are basic items you should always have. Add other items according to your family's needs. For example, while some families consider chips, cereals and snacks as must-haves, others can't be without feta cheese and imported olives. Use these basic pantry suggestions as a handy reference list when creating your grocery list. Don't forget refrigerated items like milk, eggs, cheese and butter.

STAPLES

Baker's chocolate
Baking powder
Baking soda
Barbeque sauce
Bread crumbs (plain or seasoned)
Chocolate chips
Cocoa powder
Cornmeal
Cornstarch
Crackers
Flour
Honey
Ketchup
Lemon juice
Mayonnaise or salad dressing
Non-stick cooking spray
Nuts (almonds, pecans, walnuts)
Oatmeal
Oil (olive, vegetable)
Pancake baking mix
Pancake syrup
Peanut butter
Shortening
Sugar (granulated, brown, powdered)
Vinegar

PACKAGED/CANNED FOODS

Beans (canned, dry)
Broth (beef, chicken)
Cake mixes with frosting
Canned diced tomatoes
Canned fruit
Canned mushrooms
Canned soup
Canned tomato paste & sauce
Canned tuna & chicken
Cereal
Dried soup mix
Gelatin (flavored or plain)
Gravies
Jarred Salsa
Milk (evaporated, sweetened condensed)
Non-fat dry milk
Pastas
Rice (brown, white)
Spaghetti sauce

SPICES/SEASONINGS

Basil
Bay leaves
Black pepper
Boullion cubes (beef, chicken)
Chives
Chili powder
Cinnamon
Mustard (dried, prepared)
Garlic powder or salt
Ginger
Nutmeg
Onion powder or salt
Oregano
Paprika
Parsley
Rosemary
Sage
Salt
Soy sauce
Tarragon
Thyme
Vanilla
Worcestershire sauce
Yeast

FLOUR

HERBS & SPICES

DRIED VS. FRESH. While dried herbs are convenient, they don't generally have the same purity of flavor as fresh herbs. Ensure dried herbs are still fresh by checking if they are green and not faded. Crush a few leaves to see if the aroma is still strong. Always store them in an air-tight container away from light and heat.

BASIL
Sweet, warm flavor with an aromatic odor. Use whole or ground. Good with lamb, fish, roast, stews, beef, vegetables, dressing and omelets.

BAY LEAVES
Pungent flavor. Use whole leaf but remove before serving. Good in vegetable dishes, seafood, stews and pickles.

CARAWAY
Spicy taste and aromatic smell. Use in cakes, breads, soups, cheese and sauerkraut.

CELERY SEED
Strong taste which resembles the vegetable. Can be used sparingly in pickles and chutney, meat and fish dishes, salads, bread, marinades, dressings and dips.

CHIVES
Sweet, mild flavor like that of onion. Excellent in salads, fish, soups and potatoes.

CILANTRO
Use fresh. Excellent in salads, fish, chicken, rice, beans and Mexican dishes.

CINNAMON
Sweet, pungent flavor. Widely used in many sweet baked goods, chocolate dishes, cheesecakes, pickles, chutneys and hot drinks.

CORIANDER
Mild, sweet, orangy flavor and available whole or ground. Common in curry powders and pickling spice and also used in chutney, meat dishes, casseroles, Greek-style dishes, apple pies and baked goods.

CURRY POWDER
Spices are combined to proper proportions to give a distinct flavor to meat, poultry, fish and vegetables.

DILL
Both seeds and leaves are flavorful. Leaves may be used as a garnish or cooked with fish, soup, dressings, potatoes and beans. Leaves or the whole plant may be used to flavor pickles.

FENNEL
Sweet, hot flavor. Both seeds and leaves are used. Use in small quantities in pies and baked goods. Leaves can be boiled with fish.

HERBS & SPICES

GINGER
A pungent root, this aromatic spice is sold fresh, dried or ground. Use in pickles, preserves, cakes, cookies, soups and meat dishes.

MARJORAM
May be used both dried or green. Use to flavor fish, poultry, omelets, lamb, stew, stuffing and tomato juice.

MINT
Aromatic with a cool flavor. Excellent in beverages, fish, lamb, cheese, soup, peas, carrots and fruit desserts.

NUTMEG
Whole or ground. Used in chicken and cream soups, cheese dishes, fish cakes, and with chicken and veal. Excellent in custards, milk puddings, pies and cakes.

OREGANO
Strong, aromatic odor. Use whole or ground in tomato juice, fish, eggs, pizza, omelets, chili, stew, gravy, poultry and vegetables.

PAPRIKA
A bright red pepper, this spice is used in meat, vegetables and soups or as a garnish for potatoes, salads or eggs.

PARSLEY
Best when used fresh, but can be used dried as a garnish or as a seasoning. Try in fish, omelets, soup, meat, stuffing and mixed greens.

ROSEMARY
Very aromatic. Can be used fresh or dried. Season fish, stuffing, beef, lamb, poultry, onions, eggs, bread and potatoes. Great in dressings.

SAFFRON
Aromatic, slightly bitter taste. Only a pinch needed to flavor and color dishes such as bouillabaisse, chicken soup, rice, paella, fish sauces, buns and cakes. Very expensive, so where a touch of color is needed, use turmeric instead, but the flavor will not be the same.

SAGE
Use fresh or dried. The flowers are sometimes used in salads. May be used in tomato juice, fish, omelets, beef, poultry, stuffing, cheese spreads and breads.

TARRAGON
Leaves have a pungent, hot taste. Use to flavor sauces, salads, fish, poultry, tomatoes, eggs, green beans, carrots and dressings.

THYME
Sprinkle leaves on fish or poultry before broiling or baking. Throw a few sprigs directly on coals shortly before meat is finished grilling.

TURMERIC
Aromatic, slightly bitter flavor. Should be used sparingly in curry powder and relishes and to color cakes and rice dishes.

Use 3 times more fresh herbs if substituting fresh for dried.

BAKING BREADS

HINTS FOR BAKING BREADS

- Kneading dough for 30 seconds after mixing improves the texture of baking powder biscuits.

- Instead of shortening, use cooking or salad oil in waffles and hot cakes.

- When bread is baking, a small dish of water in the oven will help keep the crust from hardening.

- Dip a spoon in hot water to measure shortening, butter, etc., and the fat will slip out more easily.

- Small amounts of leftover corn may be added to pancake batter for variety.

- To make bread crumbs, use the fine cutter of a food grinder and tie a large paper bag over the spout in order to prevent flying crumbs.

- When you are doing any sort of baking, you get better results if you remember to preheat your cookie sheet, muffin tins or cake pans.

3 RULES FOR USE OF LEAVENING AGENTS

1. In simple flour mixtures, use 2 teaspoons baking powder to leaven 1 cup flour. Reduce this amount $1/2$ teaspoon for each egg used.

2. To 1 teaspoon soda, use 2 $1/4$ teaspoons cream of tartar, 2 cups freshly soured milk or 1 cup molasses.

3. To substitute soda and an acid for baking powder, divide the amount of baking powder by 4. Take that as your measure and add acid according to rule 2.

PROPORTIONS OF BAKING POWDER TO FLOUR

biscuits ....to 1 cup flour use 1 $1/4$ tsp. baking powder
cake with oil ....to 1 cup flour use 1 tsp. baking powder
muffins ....to 1 cup flour use 1 $1/2$ tsp. baking powder
popovers ....to 1 cup flour use 1 $1/4$ tsp. baking powder
waffles ....to 1 cup flour use 1 $1/4$ tsp. baking powder

PROPORTIONS OF LIQUID TO FLOUR

pour batter ....to 1 cup liquid use 1 cup flour
drop batter ....to 1 cup liquid use 2 to 2 $1/2$ cups flour
soft dough ....to 1 cup liquid use 3 to 3 $1/2$ cups flour
stiff dough ....to 1 cup liquid use 4 cups flour

TIME & TEMPERATURE CHART

Breads	Minutes	Temperature
biscuits	12 - 15	400° - 450°
cornbread	25 - 30	400° - 425°
gingerbread	40 - 50	350° - 370°
loaf	50 - 60	350° - 400°
nut bread	50 - 75	350°
popovers	30 - 40	425° - 450°
rolls	20 - 30	400° - 450°

BAKING DESSERTS

PERFECT COOKIES

Cookie dough that must be rolled is much easier to handle after it has been refrigerated for 10 to 30 minutes. This keeps the dough from sticking, even though it may be soft. If not done, the soft dough may require more flour and too much flour makes cookies hard and brittle. Place on a floured board only as much dough as can be easily managed. Flour the rolling pin slightly and roll lightly to desired thickness. Cut shapes close together and add trimmings to dough that needs to be rolled. Place pans or sheets in upper third of oven. Watch cookies carefully while baking in order to avoid burned edges. When sprinkling sugar on cookies, try putting it into a salt shaker in order to save time.

PERFECT PIES

- Pie crust will be better and easier to make if all the ingredients are cool.

- The lower crust should be placed in the pan so that it covers the surface smoothly. Air pockets beneath the surface will push the crust out of shape while baking.

- Folding the top crust over the lower crust before crimping will keep juices in the pie.

- When making custard pie, bake at a high temperature for about 10 minutes to prevent a soggy crust. Then finish baking at a low temperature.

- When making cream pie, sprinkle crust with powdered sugar in order to prevent it from becoming soggy.

PERFECT CAKES

- Fill cake pans two-thirds full and spread batter into corners and sides, leaving a slight hollow in the center.

- Cake is done when it shrinks from the sides of the pan or if it springs back when touched lightly with the finger.

- After removing a cake from the oven, place it on a rack for about 5 minutes. Then, the sides should be loosened and the cake turned out on a rack in order to finish cooling.

- Do not frost cakes until thoroughly cool.

- Icing will remain where you put it if you sprinkle cake with powdered sugar first.

TIME & TEMPERATURE CHART

Dessert	Time	Temperature
butter cake, layer	20-40 min.	380° - 400°
butter cake, loaf	40-60 min.	360° - 400°
cake, angel	50-60 min.	300° - 360°
cake, fruit	3-4 hrs.	275° - 325°
cake, sponge	40-60 min.	300° - 350°
cookies, molasses	18-20 min.	350° - 375°
cookies, thin	10-12 min.	380° - 390°
cream puffs	45-60 min.	300° - 350°
meringue	40-60 min.	250° - 300°
pie crust	20-40 min.	400° - 500°

VEGETABLES & FRUITS

COOKING TIME TABLE

Vegetable	Cooking Method	Time
artichokes	boiled	40 min.
	steamed	45-60 min.
asparagus tips	boiled	10-15 min.
beans, lima	boiled	20-40 min.
	steamed	60 min.
beans, string	boiled	15-35 min.
	steamed	60 min.
beets, old	boiled or steamed	1-2 hours.
beets, young with skin	boiled	30 min.
	steamed	60 min.
	baked	70-90 min.
broccoli, flowerets	boiled	5-10 min.
broccoli, stems	boiled	20-30 min.
brussels sprouts	boiled	20-30 min.
cabbage, chopped	boiled	10-20 min.
	steamed	25 min.
carrots, cut across	boiled	8-10 min.
	steamed	40 min.
cauliflower, flowerets	boiled	8-10 min.
cauliflower, stem down	boiled	20-30 min.
corn, green, tender	boiled	5-10 min.
	steamed	15 min.
	baked	20 min.
corn on the cob	boiled	8-10 min.
	steamed	15 min.
eggplant, whole	boiled	30 min.
	steamed	40 min.
	baked	45 min.
parsnips	boiled	25-40 min.
	steamed	60 min.
	baked	60-75 min.
peas, green	boiled or steamed	5-15 min.
potatoes	boiled	20-40 min.
	steamed	60 min.
	baked	45-60 min.
pumpkin or squash	boiled	20-40 min.
	steamed	45 min.
	baked	60 min.
tomatoes	boiled	5-15 min.
turnips	boiled	25-40 min.

DRYING TIME TABLE

Fruit	Sugar or Honey	Cooking Time
apricots	1/4 c. for each cup of fruit	about 40 min.
figs	1 T. for each cup of fruit	about 30 min.
peaches	1/4 c. for each cup of fruit	about 45 min.
prunes	2 T. for each cup of fruit	about 45 min.

VEGETABLES *&* FRUITS

BUYING FRESH VEGETABLES

Artichokes: Look for compact, tightly closed heads with green, clean-looking leaves. Avoid those with leaves that are brown or separated.

Asparagus: Stalks should be tender and firm; tips should be close and compact. Choose the stalks with very little white; they are more tender. Use asparagus soon because it toughens quickly.

Beans, Snap: Those with small seeds inside the pods are best. Avoid beans with dry-looking pods.

Broccoli, Brussels Sprouts and Cauliflower: Flower clusters on broccoli and cauliflower should be tight and close together. Brussels sprouts should be firm and compact. Smudgy, dirty spots may indicate pests or disease.

Cabbage and Head Lettuce: Choose heads that are heavy for their size. Avoid cabbage with worm holes and lettuce with discoloration or soft rot.

Cucumbers: Choose long, slender cucumbers for best quality. May be dark or medium green, but yellow ones are undesirable.

Mushrooms: Caps should be closed around the stems. Avoid black or brown gills.

Peas and Lima Beans: Select pods that are well-filled but not bulging. Avoid dried, spotted, yellow or limp pods.

BUYING FRESH FRUITS

Bananas: Skin should be free of bruises and black or brown spots. Purchase them slightly green and allow them to ripen at room temperature.

Berries: Select plump, solid berries with good color. Avoid stained containers which indicate wet or leaky berries. Berries with clinging caps, such as blackberries and raspberries, may be unripe. Strawberries without caps may be overripe.

Melons: In cantaloupes, thick, close netting on the rind indicates best quality. Cantaloupes are ripe when the stem scar is smooth and the space between the netting is yellow or yellow-green. They are best when fully ripe with fruity odor.

Honeydews are ripe when rind has creamy to yellowish color and velvety texture. Immature honeydews are whitish-green.

Ripe watermelons have some yellow color on one side. If melons are white or pale green on one side, they are not ripe.

Oranges, Grapefruit and Lemons: Choose those heavy for their size. Smoother, thinner skins usually indicate more juice. Most skin markings do not affect quality. Oranges with a slight greenish tinge may be just as ripe as fully colored ones. Light or greenish-yellow lemons are more tart than deep yellow ones. Avoid citrus fruits showing withered, sunken or soft areas.

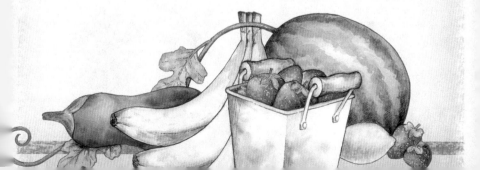

NAPKIN FOLDING

FOR BEST RESULTS, use well-starched linen napkins if possible. For more complicated folds, 24-inch napkins work best. Practice the folds with newspapers. Children will have fun decorating the table once they learn these attractive folds!

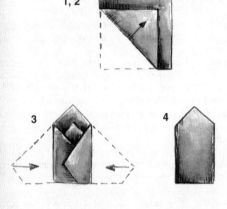

1, 2

3   **4**

SHIELD

Easy fold. Elegant with monogram in corner.

Instructions:
1. Fold into quarter size. If monogrammed, ornate corner should face down.
2. Turn up folded corner three-quarters.
3. Overlap right side and left side points.
4. Turn over; adjust sides so they are even, single point in center.
5. Place point up or down on plate, or left of plate.

ROSETTE

Elegant on plate.

Instructions:
1. Fold left and right edges to center, leaving 1/2" opening along center.
2. Pleat firmly from top edge to bottom edge. Sharpen edges with hot iron.
3. Pinch center together. If necessary, use small piece of pipe cleaner to secure and top with single flower.
4. Spread out rosette.

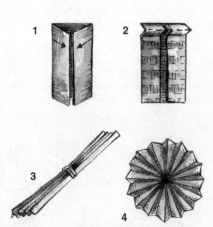

1   **2**

3   **4**

NAPKIN FOLDING

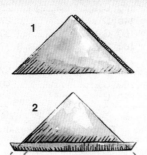

CANDLE

Easy to do; can be decorated.

Instructions:
1. Fold into triangle, point at top.
2. Turn lower edge up 1".
3. Turn over, folded edge down.
4. Roll tightly from left to right.
5. Tuck in corner. Stand upright.

FAN

Pretty in napkin ring or on plate.

Instructions:
1. Fold top and bottom edges to center.
2. Fold top and bottom edges to center a second time.
3. Pleat firmly from the left edge. Sharpen edges with hot iron.
4. Spread out fan. Balance flat folds of each side on table. Well-starched napkins will hold shape.

LILY

Effective and pretty on table.

Instructions:
1. Fold napkin into quarters.
2. Fold into triangle, closed corner to open points.
3. Turn two points over to other side. (Two points are on either side of closed point.)
4. Pleat.
5. Place closed end in glass. Pull down two points on each side and shape.

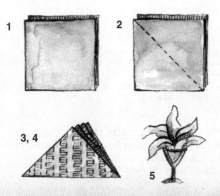

MEASUREMENTS & SUBSTITUTIONS

MEASUREMENTS

a pinch	1/8 teaspoon or less
3 teaspoons	1 tablespoon
4 tablespoons	1/4 cup
8 tablespoons	1/2 cup
12 tablespoons	3/4 cup
16 tablespoons	1 cup
2 cups	1 pint
4 cups	1 quart
4 quarts	1 gallon
8 quarts	1 peck
4 pecks	1 bushel
16 ounces	1 pound
32 ounces	1 quart
1 ounce liquid	2 tablespoons
8 ounces liquid	1 cup

Use standard measuring spoons and cups. All measurements are level.

C° TO F° CONVERSION

120° C	250° F
140° C	275° F
150° C	300° F
160° C	325° F
180° C	350° F
190° C	375° F
200° C	400° F
220° C	425° F
230° C	450° F

Temperature conversions are estimates.

SUBSTITUTIONS

Ingredient	Quantity	Substitute
baking powder	1 teaspoon	1/4 tsp. baking soda plus 1/2 tsp. cream of tartar
chocolate	1 square (1 oz.)	3 or 4 T. cocoa plus 1 T. butter
cornstarch	1 tablespoon	2 T. flour or 2 tsp. quick-cooking tapioca
cracker crumbs	3/4 cup	1 c. bread crumbs
dates	1 lb.	1 1/2 c. dates, pitted and cut
dry mustard	1 teaspoon	1 T. prepared mustard
flour, self-rising	1 cup	1 c. all-purpose flour, 1/2 tsp. salt, and 1 tsp. baking powder
herbs, fresh	1 tablespoon	1 tsp. dried herbs
ketchup or chili sauce	1 cup	1 c. tomato sauce plus 1/2 c. sugar and 2 T. vinegar (for use in cooking)
milk, sour	1 cup	1 T. lemon juice or vinegar plus sweet milk to make 1 c. (let stand 5 minutes)
whole	1 cup	1/2 c. evaporated milk plus 1/2 c. water
min. marshmallows	10	1 lg. marshmallow
onion, fresh	1 small	1 T. instant minced onion, rehydrated
sugar, brown	1/2 cup	2 T. molasses in 1/2 c. granulated sugar
powdered	1 cup	1 c. granulated sugar plus 1 tsp. cornstarch
tomato juice	1 cup	1/2 c. tomato sauce plus 1/2 c. water

When substituting cocoa for chocolate in cakes, the amount of flour must be reduced. Brown and white sugars usually can be interchanged.

SUGAR

EQUIVALENCY CHART

Food	Quantity	Yield
apple	1 medium	1 cup
banana, mashed	1 medium	1/3 cup
bread	1 1/2 slices	1 cup soft crumbs
bread	1 slice	1/4 cup fine, dry crumbs
butter	1 stick or 1/4 pound	1/2 cup
cheese, American, cubed	1 pound	2 2/3 cups
American, grated	1 pound	5 cups
cream cheese	3-ounce package	6 2/3 tablespoons
chocolate, bitter	1 square	1 ounce
cocoa	1 pound	4 cups
coconut	1 1/2 pound package	2 2/3 cups
coffee, ground	1 pound	5 cups
cornmeal	1 pound	3 cups
cornstarch	1 pound	3 cups
crackers, graham	14 squares	1 cup fine crumbs
saltine	28 crackers	1 cup fine crumbs
egg	4-5 whole	1 cup
whites	8-10	1 cup
yolks	10-12	1 cup
evaporated milk	1 cup	3 cups whipped
flour, cake, sifted	1 pound	4 1/2 cups
rye	1 pound	5 cups
white, sifted	1 pound	4 cups
white, unsifted	1 pound	3 3/4 cups
gelatin, flavored	3 1/4 ounces	1/2 cup
unflavored	1/4 ounce	1 tablespoon
lemon	1 medium	3 tablespoon juice
marshmallows	16	1/4 pound
noodles, cooked	8-ounce package	7 cups
uncooked	4 ounces (1 1/2 cups)	2-3 cups cooked
macaroni, cooked	8-ounce package	6 cups
macaroni, uncooked	4 ounces (1 1/4 cups)	2 1/4 cups cooked
spaghetti, uncooked	7 ounces	4 cups cooked
nuts, chopped	1/4 pound	1 cup
almonds	1 pound	3 1/2 cups
walnuts, broken	1 pound	3 cups
walnuts, unshelled	1 pound	1 1/2 to 1 3/4 cups
onion	1 medium	1/2 cup
orange	3-4 medium	1 cup juice
raisins	1 pound	3 1/2 cups
rice, brown	1 cup	4 cups cooked
converted	1 cup	3 1/2 cups cooked
regular	1 cup	3 cups cooked
wild	1 cup	4 cups cooked
sugar, brown	1 pound	2 1/2 cups
powdered	1 pound	3 1/2 cups
white	1 pound	2 cups
vanilla wafers	22	1 cup fine crumbs
zwieback, crumbled	4	1 cups

FOOD QUANTITIES

FOR LARGE SERVINGS

	25 Servings	50 Servings	100 Servings
Beverages:			
coffee	1/2 pound and 1 1/2 gallons water	1 pound and 3 gallons water	2 pounds and 6 gallons water
lemonade	10-15 lemons and 1 1/2 gallons water	20-30 lemons and 3 gallons water	40-60 lemons and 6 gallons water
tea	1/12 pound and 1 1/2 gallons water	1/6 pound and 3 gallons water	1/3 pound and 6 gallons water
Desserts:			
layered cake	1 12" cake	3 10" cakes	6 10" cakes
sheet cake	1 10" x 12" cake	1 12" x 20" cake	2 12" x 20" cakes
watermelon	37 1/2 pounds	75 pounds	150 pounds
whipping cream	3/4 pint	1 1/2 to 2 pints	3-4 pints
Ice cream:			
brick	3 1/4 quarts	6 1/2 quarts	13 quarts
bulk	2 1/4 quarts	4 1/2 quarts or 1 1/4 gallons	9 quarts or 2 1/2 gallons
Meat, poultry or fish:			
fish	13 pounds	25 pounds	50 pounds
fish, fillets or steak	7 1/2 pounds	15 pounds	30 pounds
hamburger	9 pounds	18 pounds	35 pounds
turkey or chicken	13 pounds	25 to 35 pounds	50 to 75 pounds
wieners (beef)	6 1/2 pounds	13 pounds	25 pounds
Salads, casseroles:			
baked beans	3/4 gallon	1 1/4 gallons	2 1/2 gallons
jello salad	3/4 gallon	1 1/4 gallons	2 1/2 gallons
potato salad	4 1/4 quarts	2 1/4 gallons	4 1/2 gallons
scalloped potatoes	4 1/2 quarts or 1 12" x 20" pan	9 quarts or 2 1/2 gallons	18 quarts 4 1/2 gallons
spaghetti	1 1/4 gallons	2 1/2 gallons	5 gallons
Sandwiches:			
bread	50 slices or 3 1-pound loaves	100 slices or 6 1-pound loaves	200 slices or 12 1-pound loaves
butter	1/2 pound	1 pound	2 pounds
lettuce	1 1/2 heads	3 heads	6 heads
mayonnaise	1 cup	2 cups	4 cups
mixed filling			
meat, eggs, fish	1 1/2 quarts	3 quarts	6 quarts
jam, jelly	1 quart	2 quarts	4 quarts

QUICK FIXES

PRACTICALLY EVERYONE has experienced that dreadful moment in the kitchen when a recipe failed and dinner guests have arrived. Perhaps a failed timer, distraction or a missing or mismeasured ingredient is to blame. These handy tips can save the day!

Acidic foods – Sometimes a tomato-based sauce will become too acidic. Add baking soda, one teaspoon at a time, to the sauce. Use sugar as a sweeter alternative.

Burnt food on pots and pans – Allow the pan to cool on its own. Remove as much of the food as possible. Fill with hot water and add a capful of liquid fabric softener to the pot; let it stand for a few hours. You'll have an easier time removing the burnt food.

Chocolate seizes – Chocolate can seize (turn course and grainy) when it comes into contact with water. Place seized chocolate in a metal bowl over a large saucepan with an inch of simmering water in it. Over medium heat, slowly whisk in warm heavy cream. Use 1/4 cup cream to 4 ounces of chocolate. The chocolate will melt and become smooth.

Forgot to thaw whipped topping – Thaw in microwave for 1 minute on the defrost setting. Stir to blend well. Do not over thaw!

Hands smell like garlic or onion – Rinse hands under cold water while rubbing them with a large stainless steel spoon.

Hard brown sugar – Place in a paper bag and microwave for a few seconds, or place hard chunks in a food processor.

Jello too hard – Heat on a low microwave power setting for a very short time.

Lumpy gravy or sauce – Use a blender, food processor or simply strain.

No tomato juice – Mix 1/2 cup ketchup with 1/2 cup water.

Out of honey – Substitute 1 1/4 cups sugar dissolved in 1 cup water.

Overcooked sweet potatoes or carrots – Softened sweet potatoes and carrots make a wonderful soufflé with the addition of eggs and sugar. Consult your favorite cookbook for a good soufflé recipe. Overcooked sweet potatoes can also be used as pie filling.

Sandwich bread is stale – Toast or microwave bread briefly. Otherwise, turn it into breadcrumbs. Bread exposed to light and heat will hasten its demise, so consider using a bread box.

Soup, sauce, gravy too thin – Add 1 tablespoon of flour to hot soup, sauce or gravy. Whisk well (to avoid lumps) while the mixture is boiling. Repeat if necessary.

Sticky rice – Rinse rice with warm water.

Stew or soup is greasy – Refrigerate and remove grease once it congeals. Another trick is to lay cold lettuce leaves over the hot stew for about 10 seconds and then remove. Repeat as necessary.

Too salty – Add a little sugar and vinegar. For soups or sauces, add a raw peeled potato.

Too sweet – Add a little vinegar or lemon juice.

Undercooked cakes and cookies – Serve over vanilla ice cream. You can also layer pieces of cake or cookies with whipped cream and fresh fruit to form a dessert parfait. Crumbled cookies also make an excellent ice cream or cream pie topping.

COUNTING CALORIES

BEVERAGES

apple juice, 6 oz.	90
coffee (black)	0
cola, 12 oz.	115
cranberry juice, 6 oz.	115
ginger ale, 12 oz.	115
grape juice, (prepared from frozen concentrate), 6 oz.	142
lemonade, (prepared from frozen concentrate), 6 oz.	85
milk, protein fortified, 1 c.	105
skim, 1 c.	90
whole, 1 c.	160
orange juice, 6 oz.	85
pineapple juice, unsweetened, 6 oz.	95
root beer, 12 oz.	150
tonic (quinine water) 12 oz.	132

BREADS

cornbread, 1 sm. square	130
dumplings, 1 med.	70
French toast, 1 slice	135
melba toast, 1 slice	25
muffins, blueberry, 1 muffin	110
bran, 1 muffin	106
corn, 1 muffin	125
English, 1 muffin	280
pancakes, 1 (4-in.)	60
pumpernickel, 1 slice	75
rye, 1 slice	60
waffle, 1	216
white, 1 slice	60-70
whole wheat, 1 slice	55-65

CEREALS

cornflakes, 1 c.	105
cream of wheat, 1 c.	120
oatmeal, 1 c.	148
rice flakes, 1 c.	105
shredded wheat, 1 biscuit	100
sugar krisps, 3/4 c.	110

CRACKERS

graham, 1 cracker	15-30
rye crisp, 1 cracker	35
saltine, 1 cracker	17-20
wheat thins, 1 cracker	9

DAIRY PRODUCTS

butter or margarine, 1 T.	100
cheese, American, 1 oz.	100
camembert, 1 oz.	85
cheddar, 1 oz.	115
cottage cheese, 1 oz.	30
mozzarella, 1 oz.	90
parmesan, 1 oz.	130
ricotta, 1 oz.	50
roquefort, 1 oz.	105
Swiss, 1 oz.	105
cream, light, 1 T.	30
heavy, 1 T.	55
sour, 1 T.	45
hot chocolate, with milk, 1 c.	277
milk chocolate, 1 oz.	145-155
yogurt	
made w/ whole milk, 1 c.	150-165
made w/ skimmed milk, 1 c.	125

EGGS

fried, 1 lg.	100
poached or boiled, 1 lg.	75-80
scrambled or in omelet, 1 lg.	110-130

FISH AND SEAFOOD

bass, 4 oz.	105
salmon, broiled or baked, 3 oz.	155
sardines, canned in oil, 3 oz.	170
trout, fried, 3 1/2 oz.	220
tuna, in oil, 3 oz.	170
in water, 3 oz.	110

COUNTING CALORIES

FRUITS

apple, 1 med. 80-100
applesauce, sweetened, 1/2 c. 90-115
    unsweetened, 1/2 c. 50
banana, 1 med. 85
blueberries, 1/2 c. 45
cantaloupe, 1/2 c. 24
cherries (pitted), raw, 1/2 c. 40
grapefruit, 1/2 med. 55
grapes, 1/2 c. 35-55
honeydew, 1/2 c. 55
mango, 1 med. 90
orange, 1 med. 65-75
peach, 1 med. 35
pear, 1 med. 60-100
pineapple, fresh, 1/2 c. 40
    canned in syrup, 1/2 c. 95
plum, 1 med. 30
strawberries, fresh, 1/2 c. 30
    frozen and sweetened, 1/2 c. ..120-140
tangerine, 1 lg. 39
watermelon, 1/2 c. 42

MEAT AND POULTRY

beef, ground (lean), 3 oz. 185
    roast, 3 oz. 185
chicken, broiled, 3 oz. 115
lamb chop (lean), 3 oz. 175-200
steak, sirloin, 3 oz. 175
    tenderloin, 3 oz. 174
    top round, 3 oz. 162
turkey, dark meat, 3 oz. 175
    white meat, 3 oz. 150
veal, cutlet, 3 oz. 156
    roast, 3 oz. 76

NUTS

almonds, 2 T. 105
cashews, 2 T. 100
peanuts, 2 T. 105
peanut butter, 1 T. 95
pecans, 2 T. 95
pistachios, 2 T. 92
walnuts, 2 T. 80

PASTA

macaroni or spaghetti,
    cooked, 3/4 c. 115

SALAD DRESSINGS

blue cheese, 1 T. 70
French, 1 T. 65
Italian, 1 T. 80
mayonnaise, 1 T. 100
olive oil, 1 T. 124
Russian, 1 T. 70
salad oil, 1 T. 120

SOUPS

bean, 1 c. 130-180
beef noodle, 1 c. 70
bouillon and consomme, 1 c. 30
chicken noodle, 1 c. 65
chicken with rice, 1 c. 50
minestrone, 1 c. 80-150
split pea, 1 c. 145-170
tomato with milk, 1 c. 170
vegetable, 1 c. 80-100

VEGETABLES

asparagus, 1 c. 35
broccoli, cooked, 1/2 c. 25
cabbage, cooked, 1/2 c. 15-20
carrots, cooked, 1/2 c. 25-30
cauliflower, 1/2 c. 10-15
corn (kernels), 1/2 c. 70
green beans, 1 c. 30
lettuce, shredded, 1/2 c. 5
mushrooms, canned, 1/2 c. 20
onions, cooked, 1/2 c. 30
peas, cooked, 1/2 c. 60
potato, baked, 1 med. 90
    chips, 8-10 100
    mashed, w/milk & butter, 1 c. ..200-300
spinach, 1 c. 40
tomato, raw, 1 med. 25
    cooked, 1/2 c. 30

COOKING TERMS

Au gratin: Topped with crumbs and/or cheese and browned in oven or under broiler.

Au jus: Served in its own juices.

Baste: To moisten foods during cooking with pan drippings or special sauce in order to add flavor and prevent drying.

Bisque: A thick cream soup.

Blanch: To immerse in rapidly boiling water and allow to cook slightly.

Cream: To soften a fat, especially butter, by beating it at room temperature. Butter and sugar are often creamed together, making a smooth, soft paste.

Crimp: To seal the edges of a two-crust pie either by pinching them at intervals with the fingers or by pressing them together with the tines of a fork.

Crudites: An assortment of raw vegetables (i.e. carrots, broccoli, celery, mushrooms) that is served as an hors d'oeuvre, often accompanied by a dip.

Degrease: To remove fat from the surface of stews, soups or stock. Usually cooled in the refrigerator so that fat hardens and is easily removed.

Dredge: To coat lightly with flour, cornmeal, etc.

Entree: The main course.

Fold: To incorporate a delicate substance, such as whipped cream or beaten egg whites, into another substance without releasing air bubbles. A spatula is used to gently bring part of the mixture from the bottom of the bowl to the top. The process is repeated, while slowly rotating the bowl, until the ingredients are thoroughly blended.

Glaze: To cover with a glossy coating, such as a melted and somewhat diluted jelly for fruit desserts.

Julienne: To cut or slice vegetables, fruits or cheeses into match-shaped slivers.

Marinate: To allow food to stand in a liquid in order to tenderize or to add flavor.

Meuniére: Dredged with flour and sautéed in butter.

Mince: To chop food into very small pieces.

Parboil: To boil until partially cooked; to blanch. Usually final cooking in a seasoned sauce follows this procedure.

Pare: To remove the outermost skin of a fruit or vegetable.

Poach: To cook gently in hot liquid kept just below the boiling point.

Purée: To mash foods by hand by rubbing through a sieve or food mill, or by whirling in a blender or food processor until perfectly smooth.

Refresh: To run cold water over food that has been parboiled in order to stop the cooking process quickly.

Sauté: To cook and/or brown food in a small quantity of hot shortening.

Scald: To heat to just below the boiling point, when tiny bubbles appear at the edge of the saucepan.

Simmer: To cook in liquid just below the boiling point. The surface of the liquid should be barely moving, broken from time to time by slowly rising bubbles.

Steep: To let food stand in hot liquid in order to extract or to enhance flavor, like tea in hot water or poached fruit in syrup.

Toss: To combine ingredients with a repeated lifting motion.

Whip: To beat rapidly in order to incorporate air and produce expansion, as in heavy cream or egg whites.